JEWS FOR BUCHANAN

JEWS FOR BUCHANAN

★ ★ ★

**Did You Hear the One
About the Theft of the
American Presidency?**

John Nichols

with research by David Deschamps

THE NEW PRESS
NEW YORK

We are grateful for permission to reprint "The Fix Is In" by Hunter
S. Thompson. Copyright © 2001 by Hunter S. Thompson. Reprinted
with permission from ESPN. This column first appeared online at
ESPN.com, page 2, in Thompson's weekly column *Hey, Rube!*

An extension of this copyright page can be found on page 226.

Published in the United States by The New Press, New York, 2001
Distributed by W. W. Norton & Company, Inc., New York

ISBN 1-56584-717-2
CIP data available.

The New Press was established in 1990 as a not-for-profit alternative
to the large, commercial publishing houses currently dominating the
book publishing industry. The New Press operates in the public interest rather than for private gain, and is committed to publishing, in
innovative ways, works of educational, cultural, and community value
that are often deemed insufficiently profitable.

The New Press, 450 West 41st Street, 6th floor, New York, NY 10036
www.thenewpress.com

Book design by Lovedog Studio

Printed in Canada

10 9 8 7 6 5 4 3 2 1

Contents

Conceits, Corruptions, and a Healthy Sense of the Absurd

"Jews for Buchanan." That's a joke, right?

Right. It is a joke to think that anyone would claim the elderly Jews of Palm Beach County marched to their polling places on November 7, 2000, intending to punch their butterfly ballots for Pat Buchanan, the American politician most likely to be accused of anti-Semitism.

Yet, if we are to believe that George W. Bush was elected president of the United States, we must stop laughing. We must suspend disbelief and accept that there were indeed Jews for Buchanan. Thousands of them, pouring out of their senior centers and synagogues to cast ballots for a man whose politics was for them anathema. The Bush campaign acknowledged the necessity of this stretch of logic when, as the review of Florida ballots was beginning, press secretary Ari Fleischer was dispatched to make the Orwellian assertion that Palm Beach County was "a Buchanan stronghold in Florida."

Welcome to the joke that exploded

Fleischer knew that what he was saying was absurd. But the Bush team knew that it would take a big lie to legitimize the even bigger lie of George W. Bush's "election" as the nation's 43rd president. Thus began the development of an infrastructure of petty deceits, outright lies, abuses of authority, manipulations of the political process, high crimes and misdemeanors upon which the Bush presidency now rests.

Like the campaign's claim that Florida governor Jeb Bush had recused himself from the recount fight that would decide his brother's political fate, like the claim that Bush-for-President campaign co-chair Katherine Harris was a credible arbiter of election disputes, like the claim that ballots cast by elderly Jewish and African-American voters were discarded at disproportional rates because old folks and people of color were less competent, like the claim that manual recounts of ballots were unreliable, and like the claim that the five justices of the U.S. Supreme Court who stopped the count of Florida ballots acted as jurists rather than political partisans, the claim that thousands of Jews intended to vote for Pat Buchanan is essential to creating the pretense of presidential legitimacy.

This book invites Americans to step back through the looking glass and to laugh anew at the absurd constructs that would have us believe in Jews for Buchanan, Katherine Harris's impartiality, or the election of George W. Bush.

This book says, without reservation, that Al Gore—lamentable as may have been his campaign and his role in the recount fight that followed—is the only American who can stake a legitimate claim to having won the presidency in 2000. As such, it invites a return to realism that, one hopes, will inspire a broader questioning of the conceits and corruptions that have denied America's democratic promise to the majority of her citizens.

It is that questioning, not the false "healing" promoted by the Bush White House and its media acolytes, that is the appropriate response to an unfinished election. How can America heal over the truth that Gore won the popular balloting by more than 500,000 votes—a margin greater than those of 15 elected presidents? How can America heal over the truth that every serious analysis suggests more Floridians went to the polls November 7 intending to vote for Gore than Bush? How

can America heal over the truth that, among the 180,000 ballots discarded as uncountable by Florida's partisan election officials can be found thousands of ballots clearly—and legally—marked for Al Gore? How can America heal over the truth that, among the ballots counted for George W. Bush by those same partisan officials—can be found thousands of altered and illegitimate ballots?

It is not healing that is called for, but rather a healthy sense of the absurd.

When America was a younger country, more serious in its reverence for democracy, the facts of the 2000 election debacle would have been the raw material of revolution. Such was the case in 1801, when a move by political royalists to upset the election of Thomas Jefferson led the governors of Pennsylvania and Virginia to ready state militias for a march on Washington. There were no calls for healing in those days, no whimpers of bipartisanship. Jefferson's lieutenant in the House, Albert Gallatin of Pennsylvania, put down the gauntlet when he declared that, if Jefferson's democratic victory was denied, federal, state, and local officials should refuse to obey the orders of a "usurper president."

That is the American tradition, a tradition that might well have been resurrected in the fall of 2000—were it not for the acquiescence of the Fourth Estate to the massive fraud perpetrated by the Bush campaign and its judicial co-conspirators. Essential to that fraud was the Republican claim—even more incredible than Fleischer's Jews-for-Buchanan fallacy—that it was unreasonable to demand the counting of every vote.

In a season of deception, this was the knife of deceit that pierced the very heart of American democracy.

I know the depth of this deceit because I grew up in a world of recounts, ballot challenges, and contested elections. My father was a village attorney in southeastern Wisconsin and, every election night when I was a child, I would accompany him to the village hall for the counting of the ballots. By the time I was ten, I had seen more recounts than most reporters will witness in a lifetime. And I knew something a lot of reporters and pundits still do not understand: that it is not only possible but quite easy to discern the choice on every reasonably marked ballot, to resolve every dispute and to assure a legitimate result to every election. Indeed, I had watched as my father and other local officials reviewed ballots, seeking to determine if marks were close enough to the proper box to be counted, making every possible effort to assure that every single vote that could be counted would be counted. Even as candidates and their aides hovered over the counting table, I saw common sense prevail, again and again, over partisan passions. No matter who my father and the other election officials favored, they recognized their duty to count those ballots based on standards of fairness and justice—and respect for their essential role in the great accounting that underpins the legitimacy of government. It was, my father would explain, their solemn responsibility as defenders of democracy.

Watching all those counts on November evenings in the village hall impressed upon me the fragility of an electoral process that could so easily be warped by those who did not consider themselves defenders of democracy. Like so many Americans, however, I kept the faith that, as fragile as the infrastructure might be—as vulnerable as the ballots, the machines, and the tabulations might be to those for whom ethics were fluid—a sense of decency and duty would keep the hand of perverse partisanship from bending the will of the people.

What follows is the story of how, in November and December of 2000, the faith was broken, the democracy was subverted, the lie became the rule, the joke exploded, and "Jews for Buchanan" set the course of a nation.

CHAPTER 1

Media Manipulation

"What we were left with pointed to a Gore victory. He was
ahead in Florida, ahead in Pennsylvania, ahead in Michigan,
and making his numbers—the expected percentages—in his
naturally strong states. Bush, on the other hand, wasn't making his number in Florida, wasn't making his number in
Georgia, wasn't making his number in North Carolina,
Louisiana or Ohio, wasn't making his number in Colorado,
wasn't making his number in New Mexico, Arizona, Nevada,
New Hampshire or Maine. Dominoes tend to fall in one direction on election nights. The dominoes all seemed to be
falling Gore's way."

—John Ellis,
Fox News election analyst
and George W. Bush's cousin

The spin was about to begin

George W. Bush was having none of it.

Yes, the Election Day exit polls showed Al Gore had won the state
of Florida. Yes, all of the major television networks had placed his lit-

tle brother Jeb's state in the Democratic column before 8:00 P.M. on election night, virtually assuring that Gore would be the nation's 43rd president. But George W. did not approve of what he was seeing on the television screens at the Governor's Mansion in Austin. "I'm pretty darn upbeat about things," Bush declared, even as each new round of numbers seemed to place the White House further and further from his reach.

While most campaigns view election night as a time to sit back after the long hard fight and watch the returns come in, the Bush campaign was still working hard. Campaign aides Karl Rove and Karen Hughes were on the phone to the networks, telling them they were wrong to call Florida and Pennsylvania for Gore. Bush operatives were flooding newsrooms around the country with upbeat press releases. And the candidate himself was tugging some family ties that would, in a few short hours, change the course of history. True, Bush was going to lose the popular vote. And, truer still, he appeared to be trailing in states that would deliver a majority of the electoral college votes that would actually decide the election. But Bush had successfully spun his way out of several electoral mishaps during the 2000 campaign—most notably a series of searing primary election defeats to Senator John McCain—and he was quite certain that he could spin his way out of the jam he was in this night.

"I was confident that, when it was all said and done, that Florida would be taken off of the declared state roll and that cooler heads would prevail," Bush explained early the next morning, after exactly that scenario had played out. The candidate and his aides understood something that most Americans did not: that the declaration of "winners" and "losers" by the media on election night has never been an exact science. Shell-shocked as they may have been at the realization that the American people were compassionate but not conservative, the Bush camp was not about to let an inconvenience like a lost election prevent them from claiming the White House.

They knew how to play the game—how to make the calls, pressure the right people, and turn the course of history against itself.

The machinations the Bush camp would undertake on election night would take full advantage of a media that have come to treat elections as spectator sports—with presidential elections as the Super Bowl. The only difference from sports coverage is that, because the networks always declare the winner before the game is done, they are always just a little bit unsure of their call. Knowing how to play on that uncertainty would prove to be Bush's salvation.

Political seer E. J. Dionne, Jr. was right when he wrote that "Americans hate politics." Measures of civic engagement in developed nations regularly rate the United States in the basement when it comes to democratic participation—with just 51 percent of eligible voters choosing to cast ballots in the 2000 presidential election and a mere 36 percent deciding the 1998 congressional contests.

Paradoxically, Americans rather enjoy election nights. According to the monitors of such matters at Nielsen Media Research, Americans tune in in healthy numbers for the quadrennial reading of the returns. An estimated 62 million Americans watched election results during the long night of November 7–8, 2000. Americans were more interested in learning the identity of their next president than in watching the final episode of "Survivor," which drew 51.6 million viewers.

Better than "Survivor" is good business for the broadcast and cable networks—which are, of course, all about show business. In fact, the networks were a lot more serious about putting on the Election Night Show—something CBS News anchor Dan Rather

The Bush camp knew how to play the game

rather too poetically refers to as "the dance of democracy"—than in actually getting the story straight. "The problem is that in the 1960s, network television was a prestige item that wasn't expected to make a big profit. It was home to some very serious journalists, both in front of the camera and behind," explains Alex Jones, director of the Shorenstein Center on the Press, Politics and Public Policy at Harvard's Kennedy School of Government. "Since then the owners of networks want major profit centers dependent on ratings. They've spent an enormous amount of money on very visible showcase talent. Something had to give. And what gave was the meat and potatoes of a serious news operation."

When network news operations become corporate profit centers, beating the competition on election night is less a matter of deadlines than bottom lines—or, as Rather indelicately explained before cutting away to election night advertising, "This is commercial television. We've got money to make here." In the days leading up to November 7, major networks bought full-page advertisements in newspapers and magazines touting their election night productions as bigger and better than the other guys'. "Election time is usually a time when the public turns to television and counts on them," explained Linda Mason, CBS News vice president of public affairs. "We want the public to be able to turn to us."

Placed in the ironic circumstance of delivering election news to a disengaged electorate, television did what came naturally: It entertained. Millions of dollars were poured into building sets, designing graphics, and hiring color commentators, as each network produced an election night "special" that borrowed far more of its direction from the sports department than from Jeffersonian democracy. As with the big game, network coverage of the big election really had only one responsibility: to get the score right. This, however, was no easy task. Unlike other democracies, the United States has an entirely decentralized election system; there is no clearly defined, nonpartisan authority responsible for organizing fair elections and accurate counts of the votes cast in them. So unique—and so inferior—is the U.S. system that former president Jimmy Carter, who has devoted much of his postpresidential career to monitoring closely contested elections in foreign lands, says he is "embarrassed" by it. "If we [The Carter Center] were invited to go into a foreign country to monitor the election, and they had similar election standards and procedures, we would refuse to participate at all," explains the former president.

Notably, there is no official count of the popular vote in the United States. To this day, the results of past elections remain unsettled—for instance, different sources offer counts of the results in the 1968 contest between Nixon and Humphrey that vary by hundreds of thousands of votes.

Lacking an official structure for tabulating the popular vote and determining with some proximity to Election Day the identity of the next occupant of the most powerful position in the world, the count has essentially been privatized. Media outlets—chief among them the Associated Press—traditionally collected results from the various states and added them together for a national count. As the news cycle sped up with the rise of the broadcast age, the various television networks created their own systems for polling voters and sampling precinct results in order to project winners before the local and state poll workers completed the actual count. Networks competed to be the quickest and most accurate predictors of the results. Getting a projection wrong when the others got it right was seriously embarrassing, so all of the networks poured substantial resources into election analysis divisions that became the jewels of their election night operations.

The count has essentially been privatized

"But," explains Sam Roberts, a retired CBS executive, "when the ownership of the networks changed in the late 1980s, everybody was under this incredible cost-cutting pressure. All the companies were squeezing the news divisions very hard." The pressure to cut costs focused on the polling operations, recalls Roberts, who talks of accountants "jumping up and down and saying what a great way to save money" when the idea of creating a single polling operation for all the networks was proposed. Old-timers in the newsrooms objected that the move would lead to mistakes and, even more painful for serious journalists, the sacrifice of control over the data that were, after all, the raw count of history. Nevertheless, in 1990 news corporations pooled their resources to create Voter Research and Surveys, a consortium that was responsible for gathering and analyzing data, then projecting winners. As Voter Research and Surveys evolved into the Voter News Service (VNS), the networks grabbed back some of the responsibility for analyzing the raw data in an effort to beat the competition on election night. In reality, however, it was a fixed race: The network "analysts" did not gather their own information. Rather, they worked from the same basic pool of data and, invariably, called the winners within minutes of one another.

By the time the 2000 election rolled around, none of the major news media in the United States made the pretense of gathering actual election returns to create a precise picture of the popular will. As the *New York Times* explained, "All the networks, and other news organizations that pay to receive voter-poll information, get their data from the same source, the Voter News Service." VNS promises to get the results of elections before the overwhelming majority of votes are actually counted in individual states, a nifty trick the consortium accomplishes by conducting exit polls and, when the voting finishes, reviewing actual results from handfuls of scientifically selected "sample precincts" to create a model of the sentiments of an entire state. This makes it possible for Dan Rather, Peter Jennings, and Tom Brokaw to look, with that authoritative glimmer in their eyes, into the camera at the very moment election workers are locking polling-place doors and declare, "The polls have closed in Florida, and we are now prepared to report that Al Gore has won that state's crucial 25 electoral votes." So confident was Rather in the soundness of the VNS data and projections that he announced early on Election Night 2000 that "if we say somebody's carried a state, you can pretty much take it to the bank, book it, that that's true."

Steadier hands noted that the VNS had never been relied upon to call a razor-close contest at the national level. And they worried. After the election, Jeff Gralnick, a former ABC executive, told the media magazine *Brill's Content* that the whole VNS system was a bomb waiting to explode. Comparing the VNS to NASA before the *Challenger* disaster, Gralnick said, "They were launching space shuttles: Nothing can go wrong. You become so secure in your own technology that you just keep doing it until it blows up."

There was a blowup on November 7, 2000. And in the dusty confusion following the explosion, the Bush campaign made off with an election.

The whole VNS system was a bomb waiting to explode

*   *   *

"We're going to win Florida."

—Bush aide Karl Rove,

after all networks called Florida for Al Gore

George W. Bush, America's first 12-step president, surrounded himself during the 2000 campaign with a team that took the mantra of self-improvement seriously. His posse of workaholics, reformed drinkers, and loners had faith in what they had read in all those "get-your-life-together" manuals. Above all, they subscribed to the "look-like-a-winner-to-be-a-winner" theory of politics. Never predict a mere victory when you can predict a landslide, the Bushies believed. The problem was that, often, the big talk made them look like political numbskulls. So it was in New Hampshire, where on the eve of that state's critical Republican primary, Bush aide Karl Rove predicted his man would win big. As it turned out, the Texan was toast, losing by 19 points to Arizona senator John McCain's renegade campaign.

Rove was not chastened by his New Hampshire experience.

As the November 7 election approached, he was predicting to reporters that Bush would win 320 electoral votes and prevail by at least 6 percent in the popular vote.

By the time the first exit polls began to come in on Election Day, however, it was clear that Rove had been as wrong about America as he had been about New Hampshire. It was Gore, not Bush, who looked like a winner.

The first real evidence of Gore's strength would be revealed to the American people with the call of Florida—the home state of Jeb Bush and 25 critical electoral votes—for the Democrat.

As the polls began to close in Florida at 7:30 P.M. eastern standard time, analysts at the various networks were busily running the numbers.

Less than twenty minutes later, the pieces were in place for a Gore declaration. NBC, CBS, and CNN called the state for the vice president within minutes of one another. By 7:52 P.M., only the conservative Fox News Network had failed to declare a Gore victory in the Sunshine State and, by extension, in the race for the presidency. Still holding out hope for a Bush win, Fox analysts pored over results from a few more sample precincts, hoping against hope to discern even the most minute ray of hope for a Bush win. But each new batch of information darkened the scenario for the Bush broadcasters. "If anything," acknowledged Fox analyst John Ellis, the new information made his team "even more certain that Gore had won." At 7:52 P.M., Ellis made a painful call—not just because it disappointed his conservative bosses at Fox but because George W. was his first cousin. "OK," he shouted, "Florida goes Gore."

We now know that this was the best call of the night. A solid plurality of Florida voters had gone to the polls intending to vote for Al Gore. No surprise then that this reality was reflected in the answers that Florida voters gave to VNS exit pollsters.

Unfortunately, however, VNS, as it later acknowledged, failed to account properly for absentee ballots and early-in-the-day voting, and had consequently projected a wider Gore win than was possible in a state so closely divided. As VNS and the networks started to realize that the actual results were not meeting their projections, they began to worry about their credibility. This in turn allowed the Bush team to play on those doubts. Their goal was to apply enough pressure on the networks to get them to reverse the call for Gore and declare Florida for Bush. If they could finish the night as the declared "winner," they reasoned, it would be hard to contest a close result.

The Bush camp's rationale was simple: Their man may have lost Florida on Election Day, but he could still win it on election night.

The spin was about to begin.

"OK," Fox's John Ellis shouted, "Florida goes Gore"

> **"We threaded the needle and did it artfully."**
> **—Ari Fleischer, Bush campaign spokesperson**

The Bush family had planned a regal election night, as befits a family that was about to reassert the Divine Right of Poppy's Progeny to rule the land. Early evening would be spent dining with "the masses" at a chic Austin restaurant, after which the candidate and his entourage would consent to view election returns with supporters at the swank Four Seasons Hotel. Finally, a majestic declaration of victory in front of 20,000 subjects—er, citizens—would take place in time for the eleven o'clock news and George W.'s bedtime. Despite a nasty cold front and the threat of rain, the crowd was rocking to a gospel choir and waving suitably suggestive "Bush and Jesus" signs. But inside the Governor's Mansion to which the Bushes had retreated, the mood was anything but festive. Courtiers were nervously tendering returns from far provinces that had not been kind to the prince. Mom and Dad Bush were getting shaky. They knew more about losing than the kid. "The old man—well, you could see the ghosts of 1992 coming back," an aide who was with the family said, recalling Bush the Elder's 1992 defeat at the hands of Bill Clinton. "And Barbara Bush? She just looked real pained."

George W. was calmer. And it was not just blissful ignorance. Despite Karl Rove's over-the-top predictions, insiders in the campaign had recognized trouble on the horizon for the better part of a week. Bush's lead in preelection polls had dwindled deep into the margin of error, an old drunk-driving bust had been revealed, and Gore simply seemed to want the presidency more than did the tired Texan who kept to his early-to-bed, late-to-rise schedule even in the campaign's closing moments. Then there had been a dispiriting exchange of calls between the candidate and cousin John Ellis at Fox.

A media veteran, Ellis had recused himself from writing publicly about George W. But, behind the scenes, he never let the demands of his journalistic duties strain a family tie. Ellis had been feeding George W. a steady stream of insider election analysis going back to the 1970s, and this Election Day was no different. As head of the Fox News Channel decision-desk team, Ellis was responsible for managing the process that would lead to the network's state-by-state projections. As such, he had access to all the VNS data, as well as a team of Fox specialists to analyze it. Ellis had confirmed the tightness of the race to George W. early on, but he reminded the candidate that Bushes always polled poorly early in the day. Democrats are working people; they get up early and vote before heading off to the job. Republicans have more flexible schedules; they get around to voting after the stock market has closed.

"I wouldn't worry about early numbers," Ellis cautioned. "Your dad had bad early numbers in '88, and he wound up winning by 7 [points]. So who knows?"

What Ellis knew by early in the evening was that George W. was not going to win the sort of victory Bush the Elder did over Michael Dukakis. "At 5:30, I walked outside to have a cigarette and call Governor [George W.] Bush," Ellis would recall after the election. "He answered and immediately asked: 'Is it really this close?' He already had all the new second-wave numbers and expressed disbelief at some of what he had been told. 'Yeah,' I said, 'it's really close.' 'Well, what do you think?' he asked. 'I have no idea,' I replied."

Two hours later, when Jeb Bush called, Ellis had a very good idea of what was going on. And the tidings were not glad for the Bush campaign. "Are you sure?" the Florida governor asked about the call of Florida for Gore. "Jeb, I'm sorry, I'm looking at a screenful of Gore," Ellis replied. "But the polls haven't closed in the [west Florida]

"Jeb, I'm sorry, I'm looking at a screenful of Gore"

—JOHN ELLIS

Panhandle," Jeb shot back, looking for a thread of possibility. "It's not going to help," Ellis said. "I'm sorry."

That was Ellis talk, not Bush talk. Bushes don't say they're sorry. Bushes say, "What is it going to take to turn this thing around?"

What it would take would be some serious pressure on network news operations that, after years of cutbacks, no longer had confidence in their news-gathering abilities.

There was no question that the networks were vulnerable to a Bush-provoked crisis of confidence. "They do not have the mechanism for making their own judgments," Alex Jones, of the Shorenstein Center on the Press, Politics and Public Policy, said of the networks in 2000. "They were dealing with campaign consultants rather than their own experts on the ground. The networks did not have anybody to ask on the ground" to help them analyze the results independent of campaign spin.

The Bush camp would speak to the fears of the networks about election night operations built on the shaky ground of Voter News Service projections. Campaign aides were summoned from the victory party to war rooms across Austin, computers were turned back on, cell phones were recharged. The Bushes were going to war. If they could not kill their opponent on the field of battle, they would kill the messenger. It was as easy as 1, 2, 3.

☞ **Step One:** Deny national reality. Rove's rosy preelection predictions were not wrong, this line of spin claims. The network projections were the problem. No, not in the states projected for Bush—even where margins were narrow, projections for the Republican were pristine and unassailable. But in the states that were projected for Gore, well, that was a different story. No way Gore had won Pennsylvania, the Bush spin went. George W. was on the phone to

> *"The networks were dealing with campaign consultants rather than their own experts"*
> —ALEX JONES

Governor Tom Ridge of Pennsylvania, a state the networks had called for Gore shortly after they had pegged Florida. Ridge was a savvy pol—a serious contender for the GOP vice presidential nod disqualified only because of his support for a woman's right to choose. He had run and won Pennsylvania in primary and general elections. He knew his state precinct by precinct, and he knew Bush had lost it. Ridge had seen the massive get-out-the-vote drive for Gore in Philadelphia and

THIS MODERN WORLD
by TOM TOMORROW

WE'VE JUST RECEIVED WORD THAT 4,098 BALLOTS IN MISSISSIPPI MAY HAVE BEEN MISPUNCHED DUE TO THAT STATE'S COMPLICATED "ORIGAMI" BALLOT--WHICH REQUIRES VOTERS TO MAKE A *PAPER SWAN* OUT OF THEIR BALLOT BEFORE VOTING!

IN *WISCONSIN*, MEANWHILE, OFFICIALS BELIEVE 2,307 BALLOTS MAY HAVE BEEN AFFECTED BY LOCAL VOTING LAWS WHICH REQUIRE *REPUBLICAN* VOTERS TO SWALLOW A *LIVE HAMSTER* BEFORE THEY ARE ALLOWED INTO THE VOTING BOOTH!

WE'RE ALSO GETTING REPORTS OF TURMOIL IN *CALIFORNIA*, WHERE NOT ALL VOTERS WERE AWARE OF THAT STATE'S "*BACKWARDS DAY*" VOTING REGULATIONS--UNDER WHICH VOTERS ARE ACTUALLY SUPPOSED TO VOTE FOR THE CANDIDATE THEY WOULD MOST LIKE TO SEE *LOSE!*

AND THIS JUST IN: MANY *DELAWARE* VOTERS REPORTEDLY HAD DIFFICULTY WEAVING THE CLOTH TAPESTRY BALLOT MANDATED BY THEIR STATE'S ANTIQUATED "*JACQUARD LOOM*" BALLOTING PROCEDURE! CITIZENS' GROUPS CALL THE PROCESS UNFAIR AND ARE DEMANDING A *REWEAVING!*

IN FAIRNESS, WE SHOULD NOTE THAT THE NEWS NETWORKS *THEMSELVES* ARE BEING CHASTISED FOR THEIR ELECTION NIGHT DECLARATION THAT *ALABAMA* VOTERS "MIGHT AS WELL JUST STAY HOME BECAUSE NO ONE CARES WHAT YOU THINK ANYWAY!"

COMING UP NEXT: OUR PANEL OF EXPERTS EXPLAIN WHY A *FEW MINOR MISTAKES* ARE *INEVITABLE* IN AN ADVANCED DEMOCRACY SUCH AS OURS.

FIRST, THESE MESSAGES.

Action McNews Network

other cities around the state. He had seen Pennsylvania's unions mobilized more effectively than they had been for a half century. There was no way the call for Gore was wrong. Yet, Bush told Ridge to get out there and challenge the projections. And Ridge did just that, pushing his message hard so as to suggest that the network decision desks might have more than one problem on their hands. George W. fanned the flames, telling reporters who were hastily summoned to the Governor's Mansion that Ridge had just confirmed to him that the exit polls were "wrong." "[Ridge is] not conceding Pennsylvania, and I'm not either in the state of Pennsylvania," the Texan blustered. Soon, George W. was burning up the phone lines to Republican governors

The line between media parody and media reality narrowed.

across the country, and the governors were giving media interviews to say that they knew George W. was winning their states—even if both the projections, and the final results, would show them firmly in the Gore column.

☞ **Step Two:** Deny Florida reality. The reality was that Gore was outperforming even his own campaign's predictions in a state that only days before had been identified as solid Republican soil. This was the big news story of the night. On television, Dan Rather was ruminating about how, "Florida is a big tamale. It's not only a hot tamale, it's the only tamale that counts up here now—25 electoral votes. He who wins Florida, wins it all." And, much as they hated to admit it, the Bush aides knew Rather was right. As Gore piled up wins in swing states such as Michigan, Wisconsin, and Iowa, it became clear that there was no route to a Bush White House that did not pass through Tampa and Tallahassee, Fort Myers and Miami, Destin and Delray Beach. It was obvious that, to turn the tide, the Bush camp would need to produce some major spin in their favor. After avoiding reporters throughout the night, Bush was suddenly inviting them to his side for a lesson in

A Special Message to the Newspaper and Broadcast Members of The Associated Press:

I am writing this unusual message to you to make sure that, in the waves of election coverage post-mortems about subsequently withdrawn declarations of a Bush victory, there is no confusion about AP's role.

At no point Tuesday or Wednesday did AP report that Bush had won either Florida or the presidency.

After the networks who are partners with us in the Voter News Service declared a Bush victory early Wednesday, AP provided this advisory to its members:

BC-Election Rdp, Advisory,

EDITORS:

The lead in Florida for George W. Bush has dwindled to about 6,000 in the vote count. A small percentage of the vote has yet to be reported in several counties, including two predominantly Democratic counties.

AP believes the uncounted votes in Broward and Palm Beach counties could allow a change of the lead in the Florida vote. We are watching the resolution of the actual vote count to assure if there is a change in the Florida results, which could yet have an impact on the outcome of the presidential election.

The AP

The pressure to join the parade was enormous, but AP people who know the state of Florida and understood the voting patterns and the tabulations we were seeing held firm, to their great credit. . . .

—Louis D. Boccardi
President and CEO
The Associated Press

exit-poll etiquette. Although his own cousin had only shortly before walked him through the details of his impending defeat, George W. was now explaining that the exit polls were plain wrong. "I don't believe some of these states they've called, like Florida."

Karl Rove was busily delivering the same message in harsher language. A top Bush aide who simply needed to ask in order to gain airtime, Rove was letting rip. He told NBC viewers that the network had acted in a journalistically "irresponsible" manner when it made the "premature" projection of a Gore win in Florida. He was even tougher on CNN, telling them they had been wrong to project the state while some Panhandle polls were still open and confidently declaring, "We feel good about Florida." In no time, network anchors such as ABC's Peter Jennings were switching from confident pronouncements for Gore to cautious hedging: "I think everybody's now projected Mr. Gore winning Florida," said Jennings, who quickly added, "Mr. Bush says he's not yet ready to concede Florida." Rove's on-camera rants were nothing compared to the behind-the-scenes blows he was delivering. *U.S. News* reported, "Rove and other aides voiced their sharp objections to network executives, who made their own recalculations and in relatively short order moved Florida and its 25 electoral votes to the undecided column." The "recalculations" that *U.S. News* referred to were in fact network analysts retreating from projections for Gore and moving Florida to the "undecided" category. Network execs could hear Rove's voice ringing in their ears as they decided how far to backtrack. And, without any independent analysis to turn to, Rove's voice was a lot louder than the call of journalistic duty.

☞ **Step three:** Create the fake impression of a clear Bush win. This was a tough task that had everything to do with timing. While the

Rove was letting rip . . . confidently declaring, "We feel good about Florida"

official Bush campaign line was that Republican-leaning Panhandle counties would eventually deliver the needed votes for Bush, Jeb Bush knew from his contacts in Florida that the big counties that had yet to report their totals were actually in overwhelmingly Democratic south Florida and in the Tampa area, where the African American turnout had hit record levels. Savvy Bush aides understood that if they waited through the night, they could well be staring at an inconclusive result—or, quite possibly, even a Gore win. Thus, the Bush camp did not merely want the networks to back off their calls for Gore, they wanted projections of a Bush win in Florida. That way, America would go to sleep thinking Bush had been elected president. Then, no matter what the final results showed, Bush would be the presumptive winner. Rove and other Bush backers hit the airwaves anew with a hyped-up "we will win Florida" line. Referring to those elusive Panhandle counties, Rove told CNN: "We have a fabulous organization there"—political speak for: Don't believe the numbers you're looking at, there's a surprise in store. The Bush push for a new projection was aided by the determination of VNS and the networks to cleanse the slate with a clear call before the night was through. Sure, it was funny when CNN's Jeff Greenfield joked, "Oh, waiter, one order of crow," after Florida was shifted from "Gore" to "too close to call." But neither VNS nor the networks were willing to sit back and let the official count, which was already well under way, take over. They would continue to crunch their exit poll and sample precinct numbers in order to make the call, if it killed them—or, at least, their credibility. Had the networks been willing to wait for the official count

> "Oh, waiter, one order of crow"
>
> —JEFF GREENFIELD

> "The viewing of the election was the highest in over forty years. . . . The networks have decided they will continue to give out false information to continue the big ratings."
>
> —Conan O'Brien, November 9, 2000

Republican spin.

of actual votes, they would have recognized the rapid closing of the gap in Florida and been able to see the signs that a virtual tie had occurred. Instead, they listened to pressure from the Bush camp to call the contest for Bush on the basis of recalculated VNS figures. Thus, when VNS agreed to reissue an analysis at 2:15 A.M. saying it was 99.9 percent certain that Bush would win Florida, the networks were primed to take the bait. Serious journalists recognized that that degree of certainty was not possible at that stage of the process. In fact, the Associated Press, despite intense pressure for a definitive pronouncement from morning newspapers waiting to start the presses, refused to follow the VNS lead this time.

Cooler heads at the networks might have gone the AP route. But, luckily for the Bush camp, they had an "in" with one of the networks. The candidate's cousin, John Ellis, who only a few hours earlier had been consoling Jeb Bush over the loss of Florida, was the self-identified man "responsible for managing the projection process" at Fox News. Through the night, Ellis had remained in close contact with the Bush brothers in Austin. They provided him, he later wrote in an essay about election night, with "valuable information." Indeed, Ellis explained, "Jeb was wired into Florida [and] gave us very useful information about what precincts in what counties had not yet reported... in the case of Florida, exactly which pre-cincts had yet to report

GOOD JOURNALISM? NO WAY, SAY THE PROFESSIONALS

The Society of Professional Journalists is the nation's largest and most broad-based journalism organization, dedicated to encouraging the free practice of journalism and stimulating high standards of ethical behavior. The group's ethics committee reviewed the handling of election night coverage by the media and issued a scathing indictment of news organizations that had failed to follow a central ethical tenet of journalism: Act independently.

SPJ Ethics Committee Says Hasty Coverage of Election Violated Ethics Code

INDIANAPOLIS—Many American media outlets acted hastily in their reporting on the results of the 2000 presidential election race, further damaging the credibility of journalists in the eyes of the general public, says the Society of Professional Journalists Ethics Committee.

"Election night 2000 was another chance for the national media to reaffirm its central role in our democracy, and it was a chance for journalists to wrap themselves in glory, to regain some of their lost credibility, but it didn't turn out that way," said Gary Hill, co-chairman of SPJ's Ethics Committee and director of Investigations for KSTP-TV in Minneapolis. "It didn't turn out that way because journalists and their institutions did not follow a central tenet of the SPJ code of ethics, 'Act independently.' "

After Voter News Service projected that Vice President Al Gore would carry Florida, every VNS member—including Fox, ABC, CBS, NBC, CNN, and the Associated Press—followed suit.

(continued)

"Not one news organization said its own research showed the race as too close to call," Hill said. "When VNS realized its error, it moved Florida back into the neutral column. Now if each organization had made its own call, you would think at least one would have stuck to its guns. Instead all six had to retreat. If each member had exercised more independent judgment, and acted less from competitive pressure, the public would have been better served."

When four of five VNS partners, led by Fox, called Florida for Governor George W. Bush based on incomplete unofficial returns, the Associated Press and VNS were among the few news organizations to hold their ground, act independently, and say the race was too close to call.

"Many newspapers rushed to press with 'Bush Wins' headlines," Hill said. "Were they basing this on their independent look at the returns, which were available on web sites? It doesn't seem likely. Does attributing it to 'network reports' get them off the hook? Not a very comfortable argument to make. If such reports were based on network calls, a headline or subhead should have said so."

Hill said Fox's decision to allow John Ellis, Bush's cousin, to make Fox the first network to call Florida for Bush sent election night's news coverage into a tailspin. It set off another stampede that spurred Gore to concede to Bush and almost concede publicly.

"Now it's time to look to another part of our ethics code for guidance, the part that says 'Be accountable,' " Hill said. "What will Fox do to address its obvious gaffe, and what will it do in terms of future hiring practices? CBS, ABC, and CNN have announced they will undertake self-examination to figure out what went wrong. Hopefully the efforts will be thorough and the results shared with everyone."

and how those precincts had voted in Jeb's prior gubernatorial races." Ellis went on to claim, "These conversations helped me better understand the data that were appearing on our screens."

Whether Jeb Bush misled John Ellis about the outstanding precincts, or whether John Ellis simply heard what he wanted to hear about an opportunity to revive his cousin's presidential prospects, Fox made the projection at 2:16 A.M. that Bush would win Florida and the presidency. One minute after the VNS memo had been circulated, and at the very same time that Associated Press was rejecting the VNS analysis as insufficient to justify projecting Florida for Bush, Fox's Brit Hume was breaking into the conversation to announce, "We are now calling—Fox News now projects George W. Bush the winner of Florida, and thus it appears the winner of the presidency of the United States. Fox News now projects George W. Bush the winner of the presidency of the United States based on the call we now make in Florida." Hume admitted that he was "apprehensive" about making the call with votes still uncounted, but the veteran newsman added, "I have no reason to doubt our decision desk."

Within minutes, the rest of the networks chased after Fox. Or, to employ an animal metaphor preferred by Alex Jones of the Shorenstein Center, "In the rush to make the calls, the networks all went careening like lemmings over a cliff." As newspaper presses across the nation rolled with "Bush Wins" headlines, the cardinals of communication sent up the puffs of smoke that signaled the selection of a new president.

At NBC, Tom Brokaw anxiously cut historian Doris Kearns Goodwin off in midsentence: "Doris, Doris, Doris . . ."

"Uh-oh," Goodwin said, "something has happened."

Indeed it had, Brokaw declared: "George Bush is the president-elect

"Uh-oh, something has happened"
—DORIS KEARNS GOODWIN

of the United States, he won the state of Florida . . . George Walker Bush, the new president of the United States."

Over at ABC, Peter Jennings and former Clinton aide George Stephanopoulos began nailing the lid on Al Gore's political coffin. "Let's talk a little about Al Gore—a life in politics unlike many, if any, modern American politicians. He almost instantly may become a tragic figure," Jennings said. Alas, poor Gore, Stephanopoulos replied, "about as well prepared for the presidency as any man ever." But it was not to be, he said.

Over in the "not-to-be" camp, Gore aides had been monitoring the results throughout the night. Though less aggressive than the Bush team, they had been pushing their own spin—arguing that Florida was close but trending Democratic. But now, Gore and his minions were beginning to doubt their own line.

Listening to the reports of his demise in front of a television set in the Loew's Hotel in Nashville, Gore watched as Fox made the call and the other networks followed. In an age of instant communication, where television does not merely report the news but also advances the story, Gore and his campaign manager Bill Daley heard the message loud and clear. "It's over," said Gore. "Let's concede." Even as Democratic counties in Florida poured votes into the Gore column— narrowing the contest to an indistinguishable tie—Gore and Daley were making their decisions based on what they saw on television. Like just about everyone else watching television at that early morning hour, they were coming to the conclusion that they had lost. As *U.S. News and World Report* political correspondent Roger Simon recounts, Daley pushed Gore to make the concession, theorizing that "in America, when the networks call a race, that is it. If Gore looks like some sort of crybaby, somebody who refuses to accept the infinite wisdom of network television, he may never get to run for president again."

"It's over," said Gore. "Let's concede"

THE WHOLE WORLD WAS WATCHING

"[A] parody of democracy."   —*Times*, London

"A day worthy of a banana republic . . ."

—*La Republica*, Rome

"It seems our virus of election manipulation has now found its way to America."

—Yugoslavian politician Velimir Illic
(who later announced that he stood ready to provide
electoral advice and assistance to the world's last
remaining superpower—and if that wasn't enough, the
flamboyant Balkan even volunteered to lend Al Gore the
bulldozer he had recently used to break through barri-
cades erected by Slobodan Milosevic outside Yugoslavia's
Parliament building)

"[We are happy to send] democracy educators . . ."

—the government of Cuba

"We could not get away with something like that in Zimbabwe without the threat of (economic) sanctions."

—Zimbabwe government spokesman Jonathan Moyo

"A pall of illegitimacy hangs over Bush's inaugural."

—*Hindustan Times*, India

"The sight of the 'world's greatest democracy' getting its credentials in a knot over who should be pronounced winner in the United States presidential elections should remind us that friendship is a two-way process. It is a shameful reflection on our continent that, in their hour of need, we were not there beside our American brothers and sisters to help and advise where we could, in the same way as they do when our elections come around. . . . We should, no doubt, have established a pan-African Society for the Promotion of Democracy in Primitive Parts, which would have established a friendly rapport with the main political leaders— using sign language in the case of George W. Bush and reminding Al Gore of the perils of perjury on all possible occasions. Before the onset of the contest itself, we should have set up seminars in the main rural centers, where the various models of democracy would have been explained, including the detail that it is 'the people' who are meant to rule and not 'the Electoral College.'"

—*Mail and Guardian*, South Africa

Daley is a brilliant politician, and his logic seemed impeccable at the time. His mistake was that he believed what he saw on TV. What looked like independent projections produced by professional news organizations were actually the products of spin provided by Jeb Bush to his cousin. Before Gore and Daley learned the truth of what was happening in Florida—that their campaign was being resurrected by the votes of millions of citizens precisely as Ellis and Jennings and Stephanopoulos were attempting to bury it—the vice president had called George W. Bush and politely conceded.

Well aware of the dubious nature of their lead, Bush aides pressured Daley to have Gore make a quick public concession. Only the difficult task of telling his distraught wife and children that the dream of the presidency had slipped away slowed Gore's course, allowing him to learn before publicly ending his campaign that he was still in the running.

Barely an hour after John Ellis had made the call that had seemingly ended the 2000 presidential race, the phone in his office rang. It was his cousin. "Gore unconceded," George W. told him. Moments later, Fox and the other networks slid Florida back into the "too-close-to-call" column, where it would remain for 36 days. Ellis was deeply disappointed. But he need not have been. He had played a pivotal role in the Bush game plan. The Bush camp got its projected win at a critical point in the formation of public opinion about the election. They had even collected a momentary concession from Gore.

Gore never lived down the concession. He was, according to the T-shirts much favored by Republicans in the weeks after the election that gave him a solid popular-vote victory, the "Sore-Loserman." Bush, on the other hand, was the president-in-waiting, who had been forced to wait a little longer by a defeated candidate who was simply not willing to stop campaigning. "I was fully prepared to go out and give a speech thanking my supporters, and he withdrew his earlier comments, and

"Our general strategy for the [next] 36 days was to convince people that the election count had already taken place"

—Ari Fleischer, Bush Spokesman

here we sit," grumbled Bush. The Texas governor's trusted aide, Karen Hughes, echoed her boss, "It was certainly a surprise that someone who had called to concede the election was calling back to retract the concession."

America had gone to sleep at 2:30 A.M. on November 8 after watching the words "President-Elect" attached to George W. Bush's name. There, the Bush campaign was determined, it would remain. "Our general strategy for the [next] 36 days was to convince people that the election count had already taken place," said Bush spokesman Ari Fleischer.

That this was not true did not seem to matter. And it certainly did not matter to the Bush camp that the reason Bush was the "winner" and Gore the "loser" in the mind of America was a bad projection on election night by the Republican candidate's first cousin.

What mattered was the spin. It made the difference on election night. And, five weeks later, it would make George W. Bush president.

Deliberate Disenfranchisement

"Do you want to know how and why black voters were disenfranchised in Florida on November 7? Begin by understanding
that this was not an isolated incident. This was not something that just happened on November 7. This disenfranchisement of 2000, this stealing of another election, has
roots that go deep. If you want to understand how the election of 2000 was stolen, you must begin by understanding
how the election of 1876 was stolen—and why it was stolen."
— U.S. representative Jesse Jackson Jr. (D-Ill.)

*"This was
not an
isolated
incident"*

Al Gore was not the first Democratic presidential candidate to see
his presidential ambitions disappear in the swamps of Florida. Indeed,
if Gore had communed with the spirits of his party elders on the eve
of the 2000 campaign, former New York governor Samuel Tilden
would surely have warned: "Watch out for Florida, boy, they steal elections down there."

The eerie similarities between what happened to Tilden in the aftermath of the presidential election held on November 7, 1876, and what happened to Gore in the aftermath of the presidential election held on November 7, 2000, read like an entry from *Ripley's Believe It Or Not*. Like Gore, Democrat Tilden won his election by a comfortable popular vote margin nationwide—easily dispatching a lackluster Republican foe, Ohio's Rutherford B. Hayes. Like Gore, Tilden appeared on election night to have secured sufficient electoral college support to make him president. Like Gore, Tilden's claim on the White House would ultimately be upended, however, by a review of disputed ballots in Florida that, after the intervention of a Republican-dominated panel that included five Supreme Court justices, tipped the state and the presidency to Hayes.

But the story of the 1876 Florida debacle would be a footnote to the 2000 Florida debacle were it not for the fact that the deal Hayes cut to steal that distant election from Tilden would define the racial politics of Florida and other southern states for more than a century, setting in place the patterns of polling-place discrimination, discarding of minority ballots, and neglect of electoral machinery that would ultimately cost Al Gore the presidency.

Gore wasn't the first Democrat whose claim on the White House would be upended by Florida

The bitterly contested presidential election of 1876 played out in the shadow of the Civil War. The two major-party presidential candidates, Republican Hayes and Democrat Tilden, were both well-educated, highly accomplished northern moderates. Yet, the race between these two men ultimately came down to the southern question: Which candidate would compromise with those who sought to uncage the forces of Confederate reaction?

When the returns from the 1876 election were telegraphed to Washington and New York on election night, they revealed that Tilden had won the popular vote by an impressive 250,000-vote margin and had carried enough states to ensure a clear majority in the electoral college. Hayes and his campaign manager accepted defeat and retired for the evening. After the rest of the campaign staff had gone to bed, however, General Daniel E. Sickles, a cutthroat character whose résumé included both Civil War service and an acquittal on charges of murdering his wife, remained in the headquarters of the Republican National Committee. He kept going over the returns until the closeness of the results in several southern states inspired him to action. Tilden had prevailed in Florida, for example, by a margin of 24,434 to 24,340—fewer than 100 votes. So Sickles dispatched a telegram to Republican officials in Tallahassee—as well as in other southern capitals—that read, "With your state sure for Hayes, he is elected. Hold your state!"

Over the weeks that followed, Republican foot soldiers carried out General Sickles's order with all the energy of minions who understood that the loss of their party's control of the presidency would shut off the patronage spigots. Boxes of marked ballots went missing. Bribes were paid to "correct" votes. Ballots marked for Tilden were smeared with so much ink they could no longer be read. Finally, when the dirty work was done, a Republican-controlled returning board in Florida "discovered" irregularities with just enough Democratic ballots to certify a 23,894 to 22,927 "win" for Hayes. Objections from Democrats in the House of Representatives to the Florida reshuffling and similar twists of the results in Louisiana and South Carolina led to the appointment of a Federal Electoral Commission. The commission's 8 to 7 Republican majority confirmed Florida and the other states for

Hayes. But the country rejected the partisan maneuver. The House of Representatives refused to approve the commission's findings, demonstrators took to the streets chanting "Tilden or blood," and a full-blown constitutional crisis appeared to be developing.

It was at this point that Stanley Matthews, a Cincinnati lawyer who had known Hayes since college and served as the Republican's principle representative before the Electoral Commission, convened a secret gathering in his rooms at Washington's Wormley's Hotel. In attendance were Republican supporters of Hayes and a group of southern Democrats who had come to bargain. They reached a deal, securing Florida for Hayes and delivering him the presidency by an electoral college split of 185 to 184.

The constitutional crisis was settled with what historian C. Vann Woodward would identify as the "Compromise of 1877." This "compromise" was achieved at a terrible cost to the nation's most economically dispossessed and physically endangered citizens.

After the southern states of the Confederacy were defeated in the Civil War, Union Army troops from the North were stationed throughout the South to defend the rights of freed African-American slaves. At a time when former Confederate soldiers rampaged through the South in the white robes of the Ku Klux Klan, the presence of the soldiers and the Reconstruction policies they enforced were essential to the physical safety of former slaves. African Americans were using their new freedoms not merely to vote but to win election to political jobs once held by the white elites that had enslaved them, and the plantation class was violently opposed to sharing power with those who only a few years before had been their "property."

The Southern Democrats who met with the Republicans in Wormley's Hotel demanded that the Republicans support their efforts "to recover intelligent white rule in the South." And the Republicans agreed. Within weeks, a plan to withdraw troops from Florida and other Southern states was implemented. A veteran of the Confederate Army was appointed postmaster general in order to ensure that patronage jobs went to whites rather than blacks. And the federal government adopted a "state's rights" approach to race matters, leaving decisions over the fate of freed slaves to their former masters.

Across the South, the collapse of Reconstruction marked the beginning of the end of active African-American citizenship for almost a century. In Florida—where U.S. representative Josiah Walls, an African-American farmer, had served as a congressman from the Gainesville area and Jonathan Clarkson Gibbs, an African-American teacher, had served in the secretary of state position later occupied by Katherine Harris—white veterans of the Confederate Army moved quickly to end African-American participation in the political process.

That Florida would take the lead in disenfranchising African-American voters came as little surprise to those who knew the state's history. Even before Abraham Lincoln was sworn in as president in 1861, Florida quit the Union, and Florida contributed more than 15,000 troops to the armies of the Confederacy. Indeed, it was not until 1868—three years after Robert E. Lee surrendered at Appomattox—that Florida was readmitted to the Union. The state Legislature had, until then, refused to ratify the 14th Amendment to the Constitution, with its guarantees of equal protection regardless of race.

Under pressure from Congress to write a new state constitution, Florida convened a convention and reluctantly extended the franchise to African-American males (also guaranteeing representation in the legislature for Seminole Indians). Even at that convention, however,

Former Confederate soldiers bargained "to recover intelligent white rule in the South"

conservative forces quietly laid the groundwork for the disenfranchisement of African Americans. White delegates implemented a ban on voting by ex-felons and even people convicted of petty larceny—an acknowledged "minor offense," but one that a Florida official of the time said, "may be reasonably anticipated from emancipation of former slaves." That law, still on the books, now denies the franchise to an estimated 525,000 Floridians and—as intended at the time of its enactment—has been used to deny disproportionate numbers of African Americans access to the ballot box.

The next time Florida convened a Constitutional Convention, in 1885, the soldiers of the Confederacy were back in charge—thanks to the Compromise of 1877. That Constitution authorized a poll tax— described at the time as "the most effective instrumentality of Negro disenfranchisement." Over the years that followed, Florida was in the forefront of implementing laws designed to deny African-American citizens their right to vote: literacy tests, "good character" tests, grandfather clauses, and all-white primaries. Tampa business leaders even created an official "White Municipal Party"—which controlled the city until 1947—with the express purpose of excluding the city's large African-American population from the process of nominating candidates for local office. Along with other states of the old Confederacy, Florida also instituted broader segregation, implementing comprehensive "Jim Crow" laws segregating schools, public transportation, toilets, ticket windows, and other public places.

In the face of racist legislation and the daunting presence of the Ku Klux Klan, African-American political participation plummeted in the late nineteenth and early twentieth centuries. Rare exceptions were found in a few majority-minority communities, such as Rosewood, southwest of Gainesville, where the voting rolls included 355 African

Americans in 1915. Shortly after the 1922 elections, in which the Klan asserted itself as never before in state politics, Klan-inspired white vigilantes burned the town to the ground, murdering dozens of residents. During this time, Florida had the highest per capita rate of lynchings in the South (4.5 killings for every 10,000 African Americans between the years 1900 to 1930).

With the rise of the New Deal and the rapid growth of the state's population in the 1930s and 1940s, Florida's old guard was confronted with African-American demands for a loosening of Jim Crow's grip. Floridian Mary McLeod Bethune, founder of the National Council of Negro Women and a leading figure in the Equal Suffrage League, crusaded against the poll tax and literacy tests, organizing night classes so that African-American men and women could prepare to take literacy tests, and going door-to-door collecting contributions to pay poll taxes. Bethune's bold activism, and no doubt her close friendship with First Lady Eleanor Roosevelt, helped her to lead a successful fight for the elimination of Florida's poll tax in 1937. But, as University of South Florida historian Gary R. Mormino recalls, "White supremacy stood at the very center of Florida's political economy. As late as the 1950s, counties such as Madison on the north Florida Panhandle, where almost half the population was African American, registered no black voters." Even supposed liberals, such as Florida's Democratic senator Claude Pepper, fought to prevent blacks from voting. "Whatever may be placed upon the statute books of the Nation, however many soldiers may be stationed about the ballot boxes of the Southland, the colored race will not vote, because in doing so under the present circumstances they endanger the suprema-

> *"White supremacy stood at the very center of Florida's political economy"*
>
> —HISTORIAN GARY R. MORMINO

"A
Voteless
Citizen
Is a
Voiceless
Citizen"

—PROGRESSIVE
VOTERS LEAGUE

cy of a race to which God has committed the destiny of a continent, perhaps of a world," Pepper declared in 1938.

Then in 1944, after the U.S. Supreme Court outlawed the state's system of all-white primary elections, the state's National Association for the Advancement of Colored People chapters launched a massive voter registration drive, a bold campaign led by Harry T. Moore, the volunteer head of the state's new Progressive Voters League. Traveling at night into counties that remained hotbeds of Klan activity, organizing meetings in church basements and union halls, Moore eventually registered 100,000 African-American voters. His "A Voteless Citizen Is a Voiceless Citizen" campaign increased the percentage of African Americans who were registered from less than 5 percent to 37 percent, creating a political force strong enough to enable Moore to lobby Democratic legislators to outlaw the Klan, pass antilynching laws, and make cities liable for police brutality.

Moore's biographer Ben Green says that the charismatic organizer built a movement of new black voters with the capacity "to affect the outcome of every statewide political race." But Moore and his wife Harriette were fired from their teaching positions in rural Brevard County, and they faced constant harassment from the Klan and white sheriffs. On Christmas night, 1951, a sophisticated bomb was placed beneath the bedroom of their Mims, Florida, home. The explosion ripped the house apart, killing Harry Moore instantly and injuring Harriette Moore so badly that she would die 10 days later. Unsurprisingly, Florida officials failed to launch a major investigation of the crime, which remains unsolved to this day. But the motivation has never been in doubt. As Mary McLeod Bethune explained with biting subtlety: "I think possibly the aggressiveness of Mr. Moore in pointing out to Negroes the opportunities of true citizenship may have been a reason."

During the half-century that followed Moore's death, civil rights activists dismantled much of the state's Jim Crow legacy. Yet, on the eve of the 2000 election, elements of that legacy continued to constrain participation by African-American citizens—not just in the old Klan hotbeds of north Florida's Dixiecrat counties, but in the barrios and ghettos of cities up and down the coasts of "the new Florida."

Florida was supposed to be easy picking for George W. Bush. A Republican swing with roots in the 1950s had culminated in 1998 with Jeb Bush's election as governor, making Florida the first southern state since Reconstruction to have a Republican governor and Republican majorities in both houses of the legislature. "With Jeb Bush our governor," crowed Republican operative Suzann Guimond, "George is kind of the favorite son." So wired into the Florida political infrastructure was the Bush family that top Democrats such as Tampa mayor Dick Greco and Florida Secretary of Agriculture Bob Crawford dutifully jumped party lines to campaign on behalf of their governor's brother.

"Meanwhile," the *St. Petersburg Times* reported in 1998 that "the Democratic Party has been in a tailspin." Battered at the ballot box, low on funds, and not even sure that Florida would be targeted by the national party for serious campaigning in 2000, the state Democratic organization was already in trouble on April 22, 2000. Then federal agents seized six-year-old Cuban Elian Gonzalez during an internationally publicized raid on his uncle's Miami home, and Democrats kissed *adios* to whatever inroads President Bill Clinton and Vice President Gore had made into the politically muscular Cuban community.

All of which led George W. Bush to open his fall campaign by boasting, "I'm going to carry Florida."

"George is kind of the favorite son"

— SUZANN GUIMOND, REPUBLICAN OPERATIVE

If there was a concern for the Republicans, it was the African-American vote. Traditionally about 10 percent of the electorate in a presidential year—but with the potential to increase their electoral presence dramatically—Florida blacks were stirred up going into the 2000 campaign. And it was a Bush who had stirred them. Governor Jeb Bush had always had tenuous relations with the black community—asked in 1994 what a Bush governorship would mean for the state's African Americans, Jeb said "probably nothing." Then, shortly after taking office, Jeb smacked Florida's African-American community with "One Florida," a plan to eliminate programs designed to help African Americans get a fair shot at jobs, construction contracts, and higher-education opportunities. Demonstrations, angry criticisms from the pulpits of black churches, and sit-ins at Jeb Bush's office could not dissuade the governor, and his ability to appeal to African-American voters on behalf of his brother was destroyed. Concerns about the insensitivity of the Bush brothers to racial discrimination and hatred heightened during the 2000 campaign, as advertisements targeted toward Florida's African-American community recalled George W.'s refusal to support hate-crimes legislation in the aftermath of the dragging death of Texan James Byrd.

The Republicans did not respond with an attempt to build trust among African Americans. Instead, they set out to do everything in their power to strengthen barriers to African-American political participation. And they had an effective tool at their disposal.

The ban on voting by ex-felons, authored by the Confederates at the 1868 state Constitutional Convention to depress election turnout among former slaves, was still on the books. And it worked just as well as in 1901, when U.S. senator Charles Glass hailed this sort of legislation as a tool that allowed southern bigots "to discriminate to the extremity of permissible action under the limits of the Federal

Constitution." In 2000, Jeb Bush and Katherine Harris did everything in their power to prove Glass right. Never mind that the number of Floridians who worked, paid taxes, and obeyed the law but were denied the right to vote had already surpassed 500,000—almost 5 percent of the state's voting-age population, representing the highest level of disenfranchisement of "ex-felons" in any state. Never mind that in the vast majority of American states, these men and women would be permitted to vote. Never mind anything but the simple fact that the "ex-felon" voting ban would deny 31 percent of African-American males in Florida a voice in the politics of their communities, state, and nation. What appears to have excited Florida's governor and the state's chief elections officer was the prospect that more aggressive enforcement of the law could cleanse even more thousands of Floridians—a disproportionate number of them African Americans, most of them likely Democratic voters—from the voting rolls.

In 1998, the year that Bush and Harris were first elected, Florida became the only state in the nation to hire a private company to "scrub" the voter rolls. Though the scrubbing scheme had its roots in prior administrations, it was shaped and implemented under Bush and Harris, who guaranteed the project a steady flow of tax dollars even after it came under fire from national civil rights groups.

The Florida "scrub" of supposed "ex-felons" was not merely radical, it was unprecedented. While other states maintain their own central voter lists or other systems to identify eligible electors, Florida doled out $4.3 million to a private firm known as Database Technologies Inc. (DBT), which became a subsidiary of the larger ChoicePoint corporation. The firm promised to purge voter registries of the names of the dead, duplicate registrations, and ex-felons. Instead, DBT/ChoicePoint delivered a disaster.

Five times during Harris's tenure, her office was forced to recall an "ex-felons" list from DBT/ChoicePoint because it was inaccurate. Yet Harris never proposed dumping the firm. Indeed, under Harris's leadership, the secretary of state's office ran up hundreds of thousands in expenses assisting DBT/ChoicePoint, including a $124,000 expenditure for a copy of the database of criminal records maintained by the Florida Department of Law Enforcement.

Initially, DBT/ChoicePoint was expected to identify voters as "ex-felons" only if it could pinpoint exact matches of names, birthdates, and genders of targeted individuals. In 1999, however, an employee in Harris's office instructed DBT/ChoicePoint to relax the criteria for matches in order to assure that no "ex-felons" fell through the cracks. "Obviously, we want to capture more names that possibly aren't matches," the official told DBT/ChoicePoint, theorizing that false matches would eventually be caught by local officials. The order "defied logic," according to DBT/ChoicePoint spokesman James Lee. But the company dutifully reprogrammed computers to widen the net of disenfranchisement.

On the master "scrub list" of names flagged for removal from the voting registry early in 2000 were 82,389 Floridians identified as "probable" and "possible" "ex-felons." In at least 6,500 cases, the names provided to the state were not exact matches. That, it should be recalled, is a figure twelve times the size of George W. Bush's supposed margin over Al Gore in Florida.

The Florida "scrub" of voting lists was not merely radical, it was unprecedented

Some local officials recognized trouble right away—especially after Harris's office in May 2000 ordered the names of 8,000 supposed "ex-felons" from Texas now living in Florida struck from the voting lists. It turned out that none of the former Texans had been convicted of felonies. Harris's office tried to save face by quickly dispatching a "corrected" scrub list of more than 400 Florida voters who had, in fact, committed felonies in Texas—ordering that these names be struck. The problem was that, under two recent rulings by Florida courts, Harris's office was required to permit "ex-felons" whose civil rights had been restored in other states—such as Texas—to vote in Florida. Harris's office never did correct the misconception fostered by the "corrected" list.

Jeb Bush's Office of Executive Clemency joined in the illegal move to purge "ex-felons" from other states—even though the courts said these citizens had a right to vote in Florida. According to Alachua County elections supervisor Beverly Hill, "They [Bush's aides] told us that [out-of-state ex-felons] essentially can't vote." In September 2000, the Office of Executive Clemency dispatched a letter ordering the Hillsborough County elections supervisor to tell ex-felons from other states that they were "required to make application for restoration of civil rights in the state of Florida."

A number of local elections officials balked at using the Bush-Harris "scrub lists." In some cases they did so because of clear legal objections—the Washington County elections supervisor determined that implementing the Bush-Harris purge plan would have violated the National Voter Registration Act. In other cases, the local officials objected because of the absurdity of the lists. "There were names on the list that I knew were not felons," said Union County elections supervisor Babs Montpetit. "One was a youth director in our church."

The order from Katherine Harris's office "defied logic"

Madison County elections supervisor Linda Howell received a letter informing her that, because she had committed a felony, she could not vote in the November 7 election. While Howell had no felony record, she did have a sneaking suspicion that the "scrub list" and the systems set up to implement it were "a mess."

Not too big a mess, however, for Katherine Harris's office to promote the list as a necessary tool. When local officials complained about obvious mismatches, Harris's office claimed that the named individuals could still be "ex-felons" who had used criminal aliases. "We were told even if things didn't match to go ahead and consider them a convicted felon," said Miami-Dade elections supervisor David Leahy. When the full details of the botched purge were revealed, Leahy would admit, "We removed a lot of names from the rolls when I know this was not a truly accurate list." In Hillsborough County (Tampa), elections supervisor Pam Iorio said, "I don't doubt at all that there were many names of individuals removed statewide that were [qualified voters]."

How many? It's impossible to know exactly. But it is safe to say that thousands of qualified Florida voters—a disproportionate number of them people of color—found dramatic and, in some cases, insurmountable roadblocks placed in the way of their participation in the 2000 presidential election.

Twenty Florida counties rejected the "scrub list" in part or in its entirety, but 47 counties cleansed their voter rolls—even as a statistical analysis of the DBT/ChoicePoint materials suggested they identified unusually high numbers of African-American voters for disenfranchisement.

Floredia Walker got "scrubbed" from her precinct's voter list. An Al Gore backer, she was turned away from her usual polling place in St. Petersburg because, officials told her, she was an "ex-felon." Walker could not convince the poll workers that their list was wrong, despite the fact that, as an employee of the Florida Department of Corrections, she had gone through a number of background checks confirming her spotless record. "I was devastated," Walker said. Her right to vote was denied.

When voters who had been notified in advance of their removal from the rolls dared object that they had been misidentified as "felons," they were given the phone number of the Florida Department of Law Enforcement and told to make their appeal there. Such an appeal required voters to send their fingerprints to the department for verification. "It started out like I was guilty and had to prove I wasn't," recalled Norman Weitzel, a Jacksonville Republican misidentified as a felon on the state list. At least 5,400 people called the department and 2,500 were cleared to vote; however Madison County elections supervisor Howell was not among them. When Howell, who was not a felon or ex-felon, complained to state officials, she was told that she was indeed a felon and would have to be purged from the rolls. Howell was in a position to clear up the mess eventually. But there is no telling how many Floridians simply accepted what they were told. It is clear, however, that:

☞ At least 108 non-felons whose names were purged from the voter rolls and who were denied their voting rights were told after the election that this was a mistake.

☞ At least 996 Floridians who had been convicted of crimes in other states, served their time, and then had their rights restored, were still dropped from the list of eligible voters. This happened despite a 1998 Florida court ruling that said the state had no authority to deny civil rights to citizens who had had those rights restored by other states.

"Many names of individuals removed statewide were [qualified voters]"

—HILLSBOROUGH COUNTY ELECTIONS SUPERVISOR PAM IORIO

☞ Though blacks make up just 11 percent of eligible voters in Florida, 44 percent of the people whose names were purged from voter rolls were African Americans. Since African Americans voted 9 to 1 for Gore statewide, it becomes clear that the purge of "ex-felons" was disproportionally damaging to the Democratic nominee.

☞ Sociologists Jeff Manza, of Northwestern University, and Christopher Uggen, of the University of Minnesota, are generally recognized as the nation's top experts on the voting patterns of "ex-felons." Using data from the great majority of states where ex-felons are allowed to vote, as well as information from Florida, they determined that, if Florida did not still maintain the Civil War–era law restricting the franchise of "ex-felons," Gore would have won the state in November 2000 by as much as 85,000 votes.

☞ For many African-American voters, the experience of being denied the franchise for "crimes" they did not commit was devastating. The Reverend Willie D. Whiting, a 50-year-old Tallahassee minister, told the U.S. Commission on Civil Rights about how he learned upon arriving at his polling place on November 7 that information provided by Secretary of State Katherine Harris's office had identified him as a felon. "You are listed as a convicted felon," Whiting recalled being told. "You are purged from our system. You have lost your civil rights." Whiting had to plead with poll workers to accept his explanation that his only trip to court, ever, had been to serve as a federal juror. Whiting told the commission he felt as if "I was slingshotted into slavery."

Though DBT/ChoicePoint officials defended their taxpayer-funded list-making in the weeks after the election, company spokesman Martin Fagan did admit to British reporter Gregory Palast that the company's massive screwup was "a little bit embarrassing in light of the election." Fagan told Palast that the company's recommendation to purge 8,000 eligible voters was "a minor glitch—less than one-tenth of 1 percent of the electorate." The problem with that calculation is that, although the glitch was caught before the election, there is no certainty that Harris's office and county officials corrected all the damage. The official margin of difference between Al Gore and George W. Bush was 537 votes—one-fifteenth of a "minor glitch."

Rev. Willie D. Whiting testifies before the U.S. Civil Right's Commission's hearings about being told he could not vote in 2000.

After *The Nation* magazine featured Palast's exposé, DBT/Choice-Point announced it will no longer undertake projects such as the Florida purge because, says DBT/ChoicePoint's Lee, "When it comes to performing work which may impact a person's right to vote, we are not confident any of the methods used today can guarantee legal voters will not be wrongfully denied the right to vote."

Focusing on DBT/ChoicePoint is ultimately misguided, however. For all of the company's failings, it merely provided Katherine Harris's office with a list of names that had been assembled from her instructions. It was the duty of the Florida secretary of state and her aides to decide how to use the materials—and to stop using them when their inaccuracy was proved.

Harris knew about the DBT/ChoicePoint crisis months in advance of the election.

"I was

slingshotted

into slavery"

—REV. WILLIE

D. WHITING

But the Bush campaign co-chair also knew, as would any overseer of elections in the nation, that an inaccurate "cleansing" of the voting rolls would tend to remove the poor, the transient, people of color, and others who did not fit the Republican demographic going into what looked to be a close election. David Bositis, a senior research fellow at the Joint Center for Political and Economic Studies and the nation's top expert on African-American voting patterns, said the Bush-Harris purge was "a patently obvious technique to discriminate against black voters" that "must have had a partisan motivation." U.S. representative John Lewis, the civil rights campaigner of the 1960s who now serves in Congress as a representative from Georgia, said, "I think there was incompetence. But I also think there was a deliberate, systematic effort to weed out all possible African-American voters and to use this thing about people being felons, sending out mailings.... The whole thing was a deliberate effort to suppress the black vote.... There's no question. There's a long history of the Republican Party doing this. They knew there was going to be massive input from black voters in Florida during this election, so they wanted to find a way to suppress this pent-up feeling on the part of the black electorate in Florida to turn out."

The secretary of state's office continues to defend the voter purge as appropriate—though its approach to the process remains unique in the history of the United States. Jeb Bush admitted only that "there may have been isolated cases where supervisors of elections didn't have the [proper] voting lists or something like that." But his office has signaled that it will no longer aggressively seek to disenfranchise out-of-state ex-felons.

In addition, the Florida legislature has quietly repealed the statute that authorized the hiring of DBT/ChoicePoint.

Pressure to Purge

HARRIS'S OFFICE SOUGHT TO WIDEN THE NET OF DISENFRANCHISEMENT

Florida secretary of state Katherine Harris's office paid DBT/ChoicePoint to help identify the names of "ex-felons" who would be purged from Florida voter rolls. On the lists, the names of those to be purged were identified by race, and a disproportionate number of those named were people of color. We now also know that thousands of names of innocent Floridians—again, disproportionally people of color—were included on the DBT/ChoicePoint purge list. This begs some troubling questions. The answers are even more troubling:

Did Harris's office pressure DBT/ChoicePoint to expand the purge list to include the names of Floridians who might not have belonged on the list? You bet. An E-mail from Harris's office to DBT/ChoicePoint read: "Obviously, we want to capture more names that possibly aren't matches ... "

But could that really mean that Harris's office wanted to run the risk of including names of people who might not be felons on a list of Floridians who could be denied their right to vote? You bet. Harris's aide,

Clay Roberts, admits, "The decision was made to do the match in such a way as not to be terribly strict on the name."

Did DBT/ChoicePoint take that to mean that they should risk including the names of Floridians who were not felons? You bet. "[Florida officials] wanted there to be more names than were actually verified as being a convicted felon," says DBT/ChoicePoint vice president James Lee.

Did DBT/ChoicePoint tell them this was a bad idea? You bet. "We warned them," Lee says, noting that the company's product manager specifically informed the secretary of state's office that a list compiled with such broad specifications could produce "false positives." "The people who worked on this were very adamant," says Lee. "[They] told [the state] what would happen."

And the secretary of state's office still pressured DBT/ChoicePoint to sacrifice accuracy in order to get more names? You bet. The list of "probable felons" provided to Harris's office, says Lee, "was exactly what the state wanted."

That's cold comfort for voters such as Sandylynn Williams, a 34-year-old African American from Tampa who, after 16 years of regularly voting in local, state, and national elections, was denied the right to do so on November 7 because she had been misidentified as an ex-felon.

Williams got a letter of apology after the election. But she did not get to vote.

"I don't feel like it was an honest mistake," she says of her disenfranchisement. "I feel like they knew most of the minorities was going to vote against Bush."

The purge of the voter rolls was not the only preelection roadblock to minority participation in the 2000 election. Indeed, says Donna Brazile, a veteran Democratic campaigner who served as a top Gore aide: "There was a systematic disenfranchisement of people of color and poor people. I think in all the years I've spent organizing, I've never seen anything like it."

As part of a statewide campaign to increase voter turnout among African Americans, a heavy emphasis had been made on taking advantage of the state's early-voting provision. In 1998, Florida enacted a law allowing citizens to show up at the office of the county elections supervisor and cast a ballot during the week before the actual election. For voters who might have trouble getting to the polls on Election Day, especially the elderly and those lacking transportation, the new law should have been a major boon.

But in Miami-Dade County, it was a major frustration. In the weeks leading up to the election, African-American activists organized buses and vans to carry thousands of voters to the polls. Yet, despite the new law, local election officials had made few preparations. Only two clerks and two computers were assigned for the early voters. Crowds of people ended up waiting for hours in the lobby of the county government building, and some simply gave up and left. "It was a mess," said Kendrick Meek, one of the organizers of the vote-early movement. "They were trying to discourage people from voting."

Still, in the face of the voter-roll purges, the troubles for early voters, and other preelection glitches and crises, Kendrick Meek and his fellow organizers succeeded in mobilizing African-American voters like never before. African-American turnout in Florida's 2000 presidential election was dramatically higher than turnout in the 1996 presidential election. While a precise calculation of the increase is difficult to ascertain, exit polls suggested that the number of African-American voters surged from 10 percent of the overall electorate in 1996 to as much as 15 percent in 2000. Those same exit polls suggested that African Americans turned out at a higher rate than white voters. And they showed that 93 percent of African-American voters backed Al Gore. Veteran Miami political observer Jim DeFede said Gore's substantial African-American vote was "the only reason" the Democrat was positioned to contest George W. Bush's claim on the state's 25 electoral votes.

Notably, had all the African Americans who tried to vote for Gore been allowed to do so, and had all the votes cast by African Americans for Gore been counted as such, there would have been no contest at all. But Florida's legacy of denial of African-American aspirations was writ large on Election Day 2000. Above and beyond the voting-roll purges, and the barriers to early voting, Election Day harassment, intimidation, neglect, and disenfranchisement served as a painful reminder that the shadow of Jim Crow still lingers over Florida's electoral process. Consider the following:

> "I don't feel like it was an honest mistake"
>
> —PURGED VOTER, SANDYLYNN WILLIAMS

☞ While African Americans make up roughly 11 percent of Florida's pool of eligible voters, the U.S. Commission on Civil Rights found that 54 percent of the ballots rejected by Florida officials had been cast by African Americans.

☞ Florida governor Jeb Bush insisted that "every voter needs to know, when they go to vote, that their vote is going to count." But a review by the *Miami Herald* of uncounted ballots from the November 7 election suggested that African-American voters were four times as likely to have their ballots discarded as white voters. In Miami-Dade County, votes cast for president in predominantly African-American precincts were three times more likely to be discarded as votes cast in predominantly Anglo and Cuban-American precincts. In Broward and Palm Beach Counties, votes from heavily African-American precincts were rejected at twice the rate of those from heavily white precincts. In Duval County, the rejection rate in overwhelmingly white precincts was 1 in 14; in predominantly African-American precincts it was 1 in 5. The highest rate of ballot rejection was in Gadsden County, the only county in the state where African Americans form a majority of the electorate. *Boston Globe* columnist Derrick Z. Jackson was being gentle when he wrote, "The rejection rates were easily enough to have affected the outcome of the election." There is no reasonable calculation that does not lead to the conclusion that the disproportionate rate of rejection of African-American ballots cost Al Gore Florida and the presidency.

☞ African-American voters in Florida were less likely to have access to the most reliable voting machines and equipment. Almost 35 percent of white Florida voters live in counties where modern optical-scanning machines are used to ensure against voter error. Only 26 percent of African-American voters have access to such equipment—

meaning that African-American voters were far more likely to be required to cast ballots using less reliable punch-card technologies. According to the NAACP, "In the 2000 presidential election, the percentage of ballots recorded as having no vote in Florida counties using a punch-card system was 3.92 percent, while the error rate under the optical-scan systems in use elsewhere in Florida was only 1.43 percent. Thus, for every 10,000 votes cast, punch-card systems result in 250 more non votes than optical-scan systems."

☞ Voting machines weren't the only technologies that divided the races on November 7. Laptop computers, which could be used to access county records of eligible voters, were sent almost exclusively to predominantly white precincts. This was the circumstance despite the fact that elections officials had been told to anticipate dramatic increases in turnout in African-American areas that could have reasonably been expected to lead to heavy demand for registration and residency information on file at central offices. In the Tampa area, for instance, 10 white precincts were provided with laptops while none went to the county's precincts with large African-American populations. In Miami-Dade County, of 18 precincts set up with the laptop technology, only 1 was in a predominantly African-American neighborhood. Had the laptops been distributed more equitably, Placide Dossous thinks he would have been able to vote. Dossous moved from Broward to Miami-Dade County in 1999 and notified the Florida Department of Highway Safety and Motor Vehicles of his new address, which, under the federal Motor Voter Law, should have registered him in his new home precinct. When he went to the polling place on November 7, however, a clerk told him that he was not on the voter list. The clerk tried to reach the supervisor of elections office but could not get through because of busy phone lines. Dossous finally gave up and went home,

Votes from heavily African-American precincts were rejected at twice the rate of those from heavily white precincts

where he received a get-out-the-vote phone call that, after some checking, informed him that he was still registered in Broward County. Dossous dutifully headed to his old polling place, where a clerk told him he was not on the voter list. Dossous waited two hours while poll workers tried to phone the Broward County supervisor of elections, where lines were also constantly busy. Finally, he gave his name and telephone number to poll officials and asked them to call him as soon as they determined where he should vote. No call ever came. And Placide Dossous, a qualified voter who spent hours trying to cast a ballot, was unable to do so.

☞ In anticipation of an unprecedented African-American turnout, according to the Leadership Conference on Civil Rights, "Poll workers [in minority neighborhoods] reportedly were instructed by elections officials to be particularly strict in challenging voter qualifications because of the 'aggressive' voter registration and turnout efforts that had been made in connection with the November 7 election." Poll workers across the state followed the directive. In Osceola County, Hispanic voters were told to produce two forms of identification, even though under state law only one was required. In Palm Beach County, Andree Berkowitz told investigators she witnessed African Americans being required to show photo identification while she and other white voters were waved through without producing picture IDs. "Not one inspector [offered] to assist any of these voters who were turned away," she said. "I feel the entire nation is being disenfranchised."

☞ There is no record of how many eligible voters were turned away without being offered the chance to cast an affidavit ballot, which under long-standing Florida law would allow votes to be counted later once discrepancies were resolved. Nor is there a record of the number of eligible voters who, instead of receiving affidavit ballots, were directed to long "problem lines," which they finally left in frustration. But anecdotal evidence from across the state suggests that hundreds, perhaps thousands, of qualified voters were disenfranchised by the failure of elections officials to offer them affidavit ballots. And, once again, the evidence points to disproportional disenfranchisement of African Americans. One of the most dramatic tales of woe came from Stacy Powers, the news director for WTMP, Tampa's oldest black radio station. Powers visited numerous polling places on Election Day to provide live news updates. Again and again, she witnessed African-American voters being told they could not cast ballots because their names did not appear on official voter lists. Powers stepped in to remind poll workers of the affidavit ballot

Frustrated voters finally gave up and went home

option. In most cases, she said, she was told to leave. At one polling place, Powers says she saw people with proper voting cards turned away because they lacked adequate "identification"—a clear violation of state law. Testifying before an NAACP hearing, Powers was asked how many voters in African-American precincts had been denied ballots to which they were entitled. "Thousands," the veteran reporter replied. "Thousands."

☞ The disenfranchisement of qualified voters because of identification or voter-list disputes was hardly unique to the Tampa area. When Adora Obi Nweze, president of the Florida State Conference of NAACP Branches and a former chair of the Miami-Dade Community Relations Board, showed up on Election Day at her precinct in Miami, she was denied a ballot. A poll worker said Nweze could not vote because earlier in the year she had requested an absentee ballot. Nweze said she had never received the requested absentee ballot, and that this was why she had come to vote in person. The poll worker still refused to allow her to vote—even though there was no question that this was a situation in which an affidavit ballot should be offered. Nweze knew how to stand her ground. "You can take me to jail or let me vote," she told the poll worker. Finally, she was allowed to sign an affidavit swearing she had not already voted, and one of the state's most prominent civil rights leaders was allowed to cast her ballot for president. How many Florida citizens were unaware that they had the right to demand an affidavit? Like Powers, Nweze put the figure in the thousands. "Many of these violations, although they have happened before, I never recall them happening in this record number," said the woman who occupies the NAACP post once held by pioneering voting-rights advocate Harry T. Moore.

"Not one inspector [offered] to assist any of these voters who were turned away"
—PALM BEACH VOTER ANDREE BERKOWITZ

WE MARCHED TO BE COUNTED
By John Lewis

People are going to die here, I remember thinking. *I'm going to die here*. It was Sunday, March 7, 1965—really just the day before yesterday—and Hosea Williams and I were at the head of a column of nonviolent marchers setting out from Selma to Montgomery to petition for the right to vote in George Wallace's Alabama.

As we crossed the Pettus Bridge, we saw a line of lawmen. "We should kneel and pray," I said to Hosea, but we didn't have time. "Troopers," barked an officer, "advance!" They came at us like a human wave, a blur of blue uniforms, billy clubs, bullwhips, and tear gas; one had a piece of rubber hose wrapped in barbed wire. Televised images of that day—on ABC, they broke into the network premiere of *Judgment at Nuremberg*—led President Johnson to declare, "At times history and fate meet at a single time in a single place to shape a turning point in man's unending search for freedom. So it was at Lexington and Concord. So it was a century ago at Appomattox. So it was last week in Selma, Alabama."

As I watched election night 2000 turn into this controversy over counts and recounts, my mind went back to that day on the bridge. For all the political maneuvering and legal wrangling over the 2000 election, many people have missed an important point: the story of the election is about more than George W. Bush and Al Gore. It's about the right to vote. And you cannot understand the true implications of this campaign and the subsequent litigation without

(continued)

grasping how deeply many minorities feel about the seemingly simple matter of the sanctity of the ballot box.

The vote, after all, is the real heart of the movement. Younger people shouldn't think civil rights was just about water fountains or stirring speeches on TV. Late in the summer of 1961, after the Freedom Rides, we realized it was not enough to integrate lunch counters and buses. We had to get the vote.

Today there is some talk in black leadership circles that we shouldn't make too much of an issue of the disproportionately high number of controversial or partially marked ballots in African-American precincts. According to this line of argument, we should be embarrassed that our folks didn't know enough to punch a ballot correctly. I reject this thinking. Anybody can make a mistake in the booth; some machines don't work; some ballots are confusing. And blacks just recently got into the habit of voting. Meanwhile, it was not just African-American voters who slipped up; the confused voters in West Palm Beach, by and large, were older Jewish voters.

It makes a mockery of the memory of the martyrs that all of the people's votes were not counted. Now that George W. Bush has made it to the White House without acknowledging the miscarriage of justice in the election, there should be a new rallying cry in America: Never, ever again! We must learn how to vote, and have those votes counted. In minority circles a Bush win must instill a feeling that people have to organize better and become politically sophisticated. We've overcome more dangerous obstacles than clever Republican lawyers. And be assured we will overcome again.

☞ Untold numbers of African Americans never got a chance to argue with poll workers. They were too busy arguing with the police. On November 7, hot lines organized by the NAACP and other civil rights groups fielded hundreds of calls from African-American voters reporting that they had been stopped by police as they went to vote. The U.S. Commission on Civil Rights heard reports of an unusually high presence of Florida highway patrolmen in the vicinity of African-American precincts on Election Day. There were reports of outright intimidation in Duval County, and Stacy Powers told the NAACP she arrived at one predominantly African-American precinct in Tampa to find it surrounded by more than two dozen police officers. She said she also saw police set up traffic checks near the entrance to a polling place's parking lot. Powers, who was a police officer before becoming a journalist, reported that, shortly after she interviewed a 67-year-old African-American man who had spoken with pride of voting for the first time in his life, she saw cops surround the man and force him to the ground. "I'll call it like it is," Powers told the NAACP. "It was racial profiling. All people wanted to do is vote."

☞ American media reports tended to downplay suggestions that local police officers and the Florida Highway Patrol interfered with African Americans seeking to vote on Election Day. Conservative columnist John Leo referred to complaints of police harassment as "a great wave of overheated racial rhetoric." Yet, international reporters who bothered to dig further were able to detail dramatic stories of intimidation. "On election morning, Darryl Gorham was driving some neighbors to vote in Woodville, outside Tallahassee. They turned a bend in the road about a mile before the polling station and came across a scene straight out of the segregation era," began an article in

"You can take me to jail or let me vote"

—FLORIDA NAACP OFFICIAL ADORA OBI NWEZE

Britain's *Guardian* newspaper. "There were four Florida highway patrolmen standing in the middle of the street, Mr. Gorham said. 'They were stopping everybody. They had seven or eight cars stopped on the side of the road and waiting. They inspected the headlights, tail-lights, indicators, license, registration, tags, everything. . . . I've lived in Florida most of my life, but I have never ever seen a roadblock like that.' Mr Gorham is convinced that the white policemen were trying to slow down the flow of black voters in a historically tight election. He said, 'It took maybe fifteen, maybe twenty minutes. But many people were taking time out from work, or going to work, and it was making them late. Some just turned round and went back.'"

Even state employees, who had worked around state patrol officers, said they felt intimidated by the checkpoint. Roberta Tucker, a state worker, explained why in testimony to the U.S. Commission on Civil Rights. In a predominantly black community, she noted, voters heading to the polls were confronted by white highway patrol officers asking to see driver's licenses and other forms of photo identification. "It was an Election Day and a big election, and there were only white officers there," Tucker said. "I was intimidated by it and suspicious of it." The highway patrol eventually acknowledged that the checkpoint in the Tallahassee area had been set up on the morning of Election Day, although officials denied that it was related to the vote.

The stories of police harassment on Election Day sounded most chilling—and credible—to the ears of veterans of the voting rights movement. U.S. representative Carrie Meek (D-Florida), was blunt. "People in my community," she said, "are calling Florida the new Selma." "Both racism and hate are a very viable part of this culture," adds Marvin Davie, a veteran of the civil rights movement of the

"It was racial profiling. All people wanted to do is vote"

—RADIO REPORTER STACY POWERS

1950s and 1960s. "When you go into that ballot box, the black man has the same power as the white man, so the white man will use all his money and all his power to stop the black man getting there."

Kandy Wells also made the historical connection. An African-American woman from Tampa, she registered to vote in September, only to find her name missing from the voter list on November 7. Shocking? Not in Florida. "You've got to remember that only 40 or 50 years ago blacks couldn't vote," explains Wells. "Things like this have been happening in Florida all along. It's just that this time it's so close and they got caught."

But, more than three decades after the enactment of the Voting Rights Act, and in one of the most culturally diverse states in the nation, didn't Carrie Meek, Marvin Davie, Kandy Wells, Darryl Gorham, Adora Obi Nweze, Placide Dossous, and the other African-American citizens of Florida have a right to vote with the same ease and confidence as white voters?

Some Republicans obviously don't think so. Union activist Jonathan Rosenblum recalled that when African Americans rallied in West Palm Beach last November to demand that their votes be counted, they were greeted by conservative counter-protesters chanting "Go back to Africa." Jeb Bush's response was more genteel. The Florida governor said that while, yes, there were problems in minority precincts on Election Day, he did not have any reason to believe there had been intentional wrongdoing. He told the U.S. Commission on Civil Rights that he saw no need to investigate evidence suggesting that thousands of African-American voters in his state had been disenfranchised. The commission felt otherwise. It released a 167-page report that found that the Florida presidential vote overseen by Jeb Bush and Katherine Harris was marked by

"People in my community are calling Florida the new Selma"

—U.S. Rep. Carrie Meek

The Florida
vote was
marked by
"injustice,
ineptitude
and in-
efficiency"
—U.S.
COMMISSION ON
CIVIL RIGHTS

"injustice, ineptitude, and inefficiency... The disenfranchisement was not isolated or episodic. State officials failed to fulfill their duties in a manner that would prevent this disenfranchisement," the commission continued. "Despite the closeness of the election, it was widespread voter disenfranchisement and not the dead-heat contest that was the extraordinary feature in the Florida election."

CHAPTER 3

The Count That Couldn't Count

In the summer of 1989, Kimball Brace, the president of Election Data Services, Inc., and a man highly regarded for his expertise on the strengths and weaknesses of election systems, expressed his fears about commonly used voting machines and procedures that fail to produce accurate counts of citizen sentiments.

"We're waiting for a volcano to erupt, in the form of a major election scandal," Brace told a reporter. "We know it's going to happen, but we don't know when or how we're going to handle it."

Eleven years later, the volcano erupted in Florida.

Florida secretary of state Katherine Harris's Division of Elections certified 11 different voting systems for Florida counties to use in the November 7, 2000, presidential election. They ranged from the infamous punch-cards-with-chads of Palm Beach County to state-of-the-art optical scan systems in the state's wealthiest counties to clunky old voting machines and, in north Florida's tiny Union County, paper ballots.

"We're waiting for a volcano to erupt"

Incredibly, none of those systems provided an accurate report of presidential preferences on that fated Election Day. While there is no doubt that a clear plurality of Florida voters went to the polls on November 7 intending to cast a ballot for Al Gore, the systems set up to tabulate those votes failed. Again, and again, and again.

Most Americans remain unaware of the extent of that failure because of the disjointed response to the collapse of the count. Politicians—including Al Gore and his aides—as well as the media missed the most dramatic story of what happened in Florida, and with it the true explanation for why the Bush camp so vehemently opposed a full manual recount of disputed ballots. The explanation is simple: Such a recount, performed properly, would have revealed a Gore victory.

It also would have proved, beyond any question, that Florida election officials—from Governor Jeb Bush and Secretary of State Harris to most of the 67 county elections supervisors—failed to meet the most basic of their responsibilities: Choosing voting systems that accurately count ballots, administering an election using those systems, and then providing results that reflect the will of the electorate.

A strategic decision by the Gore campaign to focus on the problem-plagued count in the counties of Palm Beach, Broward, and Miami-Dade created the impression that voting systems and ballot designs in those counties were the most flawed. They were certainly flawed, particularly in Palm Beach County—a jurisdiction so epic in its missteps that it merits a chapter of its own. But if we adopt the generally accepted principle that the best voting system is the one that most accurately records the highest proportion of votes, then Palm Beach was a pinnacle of precision compared with much of Florida.

A survey of county election supervisors conducted a week after the election revealed that 15 Florida counties had higher ballot rejection rates than Palm Beach County. The worst was Gadsden County, which used a relatively sophisticated and generally well regarded optical scanning system. A whopping 12.4 percent of all ballots cast for president in that Florida panhandle county went uncounted—2,085 out of 16,812. That means that 1 out of every 8 votes cast in Gadsden County was discarded.

By comparison, the discard rate in Palm Beach County was 6.43 percent, in Miami-Dade 4.37 percent, and in Broward just 2.49 percent—a figure below the state average of 3 percent and close to the national average.

Election officials in Florida, from Governor Bush and Secretary of State Harris down to local election board chairs, loudly defended their voting systems during the 36-day imbroglio that followed Florida's attempt at an election on November 7. If there were problems, the official line was, blame the voters. "It was a long ballot, and we may have some voters up here who don't take the time to inform themselves," allowed Gadsden County Supervisor of Elections Denny Hutchinson. Republican operatives and their media acolytes were only too happy to foster the illusion that the only trashed ballots were those of citizens too ignorant or infirm to perform the simple task of voting. Asked why 22,000 ballots were discarded in Florida's Duval County—more than half of them from Democrat-leaning, predominantly African-American precincts in the city of Jacksonville—Mike Hightower, the Bush campaign's northeast Florida chair, said, "I have no idea why 22,000 people could not follow directions." Conservative commentator Ann Coulter described confused Florida voters as "stupid," "feeble-minded," and "jackasses." Fox television personality Bill O'Reilly summed up the Bush campaign spin when he said of voters who complained about flawed voting systems and ballot designs: "They're morons. . . . I mean, what are you supposed to do? Are you supposed to go in and pull the ballot for them?"

Palm Beach was a pinnacle of precision compared with much of Florida

In fact, O'Reilly was the moron. His comment illustrated fundamental ignorance of the Florida dynamic, in that he spoke of pulling the ballot—an apparent reference to pulling the lever on voting machines that, while commonly used in the northeastern United States, were used in only one Florida county on November 7. He displayed an even greater ignorance by suggesting that poll workers are not supposed to help voters "pull the ballot" or otherwise assure that the sentiment of the confused citizen is registered—in fact, poll workers are required by law to do just that.

O'Reilly's moronic outburst flew in the face of the general sentiment of veteran poll watchers and academic experts on voting, who say flawed voting systems and ballot designs—not voter incompetence— were at the root of the mess in Florida. "Are these stupid voters? Or is it a stupid voting system?" asked University of California–Berkeley professor Henry Brady. "There's certainly evidence here that these were not stupid voters."

The American Association of Public Opinion Research's Don A. Dillman, a specialist on the design of paper questionnaires, reviewed one Florida ballot design and said, "I've never seen one set up like this. It's very confusing the way they have put things on the right side together with things on the left side. I can see why there might be a problem. If you passed over the first candidate to go for the second candidate, it's logical that you'd punch the second hole." Dr. Jakob Nielsen, perhaps the world's most widely recognized expert in issues of technology design and use, may have put it best when he wrote, "When people have problems using a design, it's not because they are stupid. It's because the design is too difficult."

So what happens when voting systems and ballot designs go wrong? After Katherine Harris hastily certified a win for Bush and a 5 to 4 majority on the U.S. Supreme Court forestalled any further official

Some of the Loving Voices of "Compassionate Conservatism"

ANN COULTER "I love these jackasses claiming they meant to vote for Gore but—whoops!—slipped and pulled the lever for Buchanan instead! Oh really. Let's pretend that's true. Sorry, but that's one of the disabilities of being a political party that preys on the stupid. Sometimes your 'base' forgets it's Election Day, too. Live by demagoguing to the feebleminded, die by demagoguing to the feebleminded."

WESLEY PRUDEN (*Washington Times* editor): "These people couldn't get an order straight at Denny's. They're demanding a new election, but anyone who can't find a punch hole with an arrow shouldn't be voting in the first place. How do they find their way out of bed?"

DEBRA SAUNDERS "It's hard to figure which is more disturbing: the fact that many of these people drive automobiles, even though they can't follow an arrow, or that so many people have been willing to go on television to admit that they misunderstood simple instructions, voted twice in the presidential election, and didn't bother to correct their mistakes at the polling place."

MONA CHAREN "If you weren't competent enough to vote correctly, your vote does not deserve to be counted. In an ideal world, no irregularities would mar voting in any part of the nation. But democracy is a messy business even in the best of countries, and so fraud and cheating do happen. But to undo an election based upon vote fraud or cheating is to open a can of worms."

(REPUBLICAN)

GEORGE W. BUSH
For President

DICK CHENEY
For Vice President

(DEMOCRATIC)

AL GORE
For President

JOE LIEBERMAN
For Vice President

review of the ballots, embittered Democrats, amateur historians, and newspapers from Florida and around the country—notably the *Orlando Sentinel*, the Fort Lauderdale *Sun-Sentinel*, the *Palm Beach Post*, the *Miami Herald*, the *Tallahassee Democrat*, *USA Today*, the *New York Times*, and the *Los Angeles Times*—performed pieces of the task that Florida elections officials failed to complete. They examined voting systems, ballot designs, and counts. What they found amounts to a sweeping indictment of the election systems and ballot designs that made George W. Bush president:

☞ After a five-month review of 171,908 discarded ballots conducted for *USA Today*, the *Miami Herald* and Knight-Ridder newspapers, *USA Today* offered this conclusion on its front page: "Who does it appear most voters intended to vote for? Answer: Gore." Had voter intentions been reflected in the final count, the newspaper acknowledged, the Democratic nominee would have "decisively won Florida and the White House." What went wrong? "Gore's best chance to win was lost before the ballots were counted," according to the review. "Voters' confusion with ballot instruction and design and voting machines appears to have changed the course of U.S. history."

☞ While much has been made of the 60,647 "undervotes" that Gore aides and media organizations scrutinized for evidence of unregistered sentiments, more than 110,000 Florida ballots were rejected as "overvotes"—meaning they supposedly contained votes for more than one candidate. Kimball Brace, whose Washington consulting firm specializes in election administration, looked at that number and said, "There is something seriously wrong with what took place in Florida." Indeed, he called the figure "stunning." More than 60 percent of discarded ballots in Florida were reported to be overvotes. But overvoting was not a Florida-wide phenomenon. Overvotes were three times as likely in counties that used punch cards. Indeed, while only 25 of Florida's 67 counties employ punch-card technologies, 83 percent of all rejected ballots came from those counties. The Bush campaign fought hard, and successfully, in court to prevent any review of "overvotes," and wisely so, as the counties using punch-card systems were the most populous and most Democratic in the state. When the *Miami Herald* finally did examine the overvoted ballots, it discovered that roughly 3 percent of them revealed a clear choice. These ballots favored Gore over Bush 1,871 to 1,189. That, readers will note, adds 682 votes to Gore's total —wiping out the 537-vote "win" Katherine Harris certified for Bush. But, despite the Bush campaign spin that said all the ballots had been counted, these ballots were never reviewed by election officials—not on election night, not during the weeks of contention over Florida, never. Tens of thousands of additional overvotes were votes for more than one candidate. These confused ballots—when scientifically reviewed—reveal the extent to which bad voting systems robbed Gore's total. Where voters cast ballots for more than one candidate—usually as a result of confusing ballot design and instructions—76 percent cast one

ACTUAL BALLOT DISCARDED
AS AN "OVERVOTE"

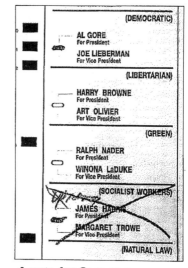

A vote for Gore or a very
emphatic "wrong" vote?

of their votes for Gore, while only 34 percent cast one of their votes for Bush. The most common overvote combination? Gore and Buchanan. "There's a pretty clear pattern from these ballots," says University of California–Irvine political scientist Anthony Salvanto, a specialist in computerized analysis of voting patterns who reviewed the overvotes. "Most of these people went to the polls to vote for Gore."

☞ Everyone has had a good laugh about Palm Beach County's so-called butterfly ballot, which lined up the names of candidates on two facing pages and then invited voters to poke holes in a center margin—creating the "Jews-for-Buchanan" phenomenon and fostering that county's troubling 6.49 percent ballot rejection rate. But the butterfly did not soar alone. A number of other counties used so-called caterpillar ballots, on which the listing of the names of the candidates for president began in one column and then wrapped—caterpillarlike—into another column or, in some cases, onto another ballot page altogether. Poorly worded ballot instructions are blamed for leading tens of thousands of citizens to mismark these ballots. In Duval County (Jacksonville and surrounding communities), for instance, a caterpillar ballot listed presidential candidates across two pages with an instruction to vote on every page; 22,000 citizens followed the instructions, and their votes were not counted. Duval County had three times as many overvotes in 2000 as in 1996, and its overvote rate was 90 times the national average for jurisdictions using punch-card ballots. More than half the overvotes—12,000 ballots—came from a handful of Jacksonville precincts where the population was predominantly African American and where the population was overwhelmingly Democratic. Those precincts also registered a disproportionate number of the county's 5,000 "undervotes"—ballots on which voters mysteriously registered no preference for president. Why didn't the Gore campaign seek a full review of Duval County ballots? When Gore's area campaign chair, Mike Langton, asked on the day after the election for the number of Jacksonville-area ballots that had been discarded, he says he was told by John Stafford, the Republican Duval County supervisor of elections, that there were "not that many, two or three hundred." Believing the local official, Gore aides pushed elsewhere for the limited number of recounts they thought they could secure.

☞ Duval County was just one of more than a dozen Florida counties that employed a two-page caterpillar ballot. The two-page ballot was designed by Hart InterCivic, an Austin, Texas, firm that bills itself as "a leader in providing products and services that help redefine the relationship between state and local governments and the citizens they serve." According to the *Chicago Tribune*, Hart InterCivic followed a format dictated by the office of Secretary of State Harris, a Bush campaign co-chair, along with a state election law written when paper ballots were the norm. But in other states, such as Colorado and Washington, election officials carefully avoided two-column ballots. As John Pearson, a Washington State elections official, told the *Tribune*, "That's just something experience has taught us you don't do. You don't split them by page or by column because you are inviting overvotes when you do that." As it happened, a review by the *Tribune* of ballots from counties that split the list of presidential candidates over two pages found that, "On Election Day, 2,416 voters picked Gore in the first column and

Ambiguity is in the eye of the beholder.

[Workers World Party candidate Monica] Moorehead or [Constitution Party candidate Howard] Phillips in the second column. That disqualified the ballots as overvotes because the machine detected more than one vote in the same race. In addition, 1,852 voters chose Bush in the first column and Moorehead or Phillips in the second column. Had only the first column's votes been counted, the invalidated ballots would have swung a net 564 votes to Gore in the 15 counties."

☞ A caterpillar ballot in Gadsden County featured two columns of candidate names: the first with Gore, Bush, Nader, Buchanan and others; the second with Howard Phillips of the Constitution Party and Monica Moorehead of the Workers World Party. A ballot instruction advised citizens to "vote for group," and more than 12 percent of all voters in the county did just that—choosing one candidate in the first group and one in the second. Of a total of 16,587 ballots cast in Gadsden County, 2,085 were tossed as "overvotes." Gadsden is Florida's only majority African-American county and voted 2 to 1 for Gore. Some voters were so determined to back Gore that they voted for him in the first column and then wrote the Democratic nominee's name or that of Democratic vice presidential candidate Joe Lieberman into the second column. Those ballots were rejected by election officials as overvotes. "I don't know why people vote the way they vote," Gadsden County supervisor of elections Denny Hutchinson told a local reporter. Hutchinson, who is white and who was voted out of office last fall, refused to answer questions about ballot design flaws. "I don't want to comment on that," he said. "I'm out of here."

☞ Many of the 26 counties that used "state-of-the-art" optical-scan equipment—which was designed to spot mismarked ballots, reject them, and permit citizens to cast a proper vote—actually had higher error rates than counties with older and supposedly more fallible equipment. Why?

Because in several counties officials deliberately disabled the function that allowed the machines to instantly spit out flawed ballots and permit voters to cast proper ones. In Escambia County, officials said they disabled the function in order to save money. Extra ballots cost 23 cents apiece, they explained, and by disabling the machines they avoided the expenses that would have been incurred had they allowed voters a second chance. More than 4,300 ballots were rejected in Escambia County. In Manatee County, where the error-spotting function on the machines was also disabled, another 1,400 ballots were rejected. In all, according to a review by the *Orlando Sentinel,* as many as 12,000 Florida voters lost their opportunity to have their sentiments registered because optical-scan machines "fell far short of their vote-saving potential." Which candidate was hurt when election workers tinkered with the machines to save money or otherwise limit their functions? "Whatever the reason for them, the errors tended to hurt black voters and Democrats the worst," wrote the *Sentinel*'s Roger Roy and David Damron. "In precincts with optical scanners, only 9 percent of the registered voters are black. But in the 64 precincts where the uncounted vote rate was the worst, 50 percent of the registered voters are black. Nearly 3,300 of the 37,000 votes cast in those precincts were uncounted. Because the precincts are also 72 percent Democratic, many of those lost votes would likely have gone to Democrat Al Gore had they been salvaged."

☞ In the Orlando area, the error-spotting function on the optical-scan equipment was operational on Election Day. But that didn't mean that every vote counted. In the predominantly African American Catalina Isles neighborhood, 79 of the 847 votes cast were rejected as

In several counties officials deliberately disabled the function that allowed machines to reject mismarked ballots on the spot, so that voters could cast proper ones

Another example of
impossible-to-discern
voter intent.

"overvotes." That was the highest rate in the county; indeed, while the neighborhood's precinct was 1 of 231 in Orange County, it produced more than 12 percent of the county's total number of overvotes. "Why so many junked ballots in one place?" asked a consortium of newspapers. "It's no mystery. An *Orlando Sentinel* review of election records found that in every instance in which the Precinct 605 ballot machine warned of a mismarked ballot, a poll worker simply punched an override button rather than returning the ballot to the voter." Orange County election officials were able to identify 63 of the precinct's overvoted ballots. Fifty-eight included Gore's name among the marked choices. Seven included Bush's name—and on two of the "Bush" ballots, the indication of a vote for the Republican candidate had been carefully scribbled over by the voter.

☞ Voters frequently attempted to correct mistakes on ballots—only to have ballots that indicated a clear intent disqualified as "overvotes" by local election officials. A *Miami Herald* review of discarded Florida ballots found 1,393 on which voters had initially marked more than one name and then crossed out all but one of the marks; these ballots favored Gore 863 to 530.

☞ More than 1,500 Florida voters went out of their way to make their sentiments clear to vote counters by marking the name of the candidate they supported and then penciling in the same candidate's name in the space allotted for "write-ins." Machines then rejected the ballots as "overvotes." These uncounted ballots favored Gore 921 to 606. In Lake County alone, 122 ballots that included a vote for Gore and a write-in for Gore were tossed out. Informed of the discarded Lake County ballots, Florida State Association of Supervisors of Elections lawyer Ron Labasky said officials in the county were wrong. "It should be counted," argued Labasky, noting that Florida election rules include a provision for recording voter choices on just such ballots. Because of missteps by local officials, the ballots were not counted.

☞ Federal law requires that election officials provide Spanish-language ballots in counties where more than 5 percent of the voting-age population is Hispanic. Yet, in Osceola County, where Hispanics make up 20 percent of the county's 94,674 registered voters, no provision was made for Spanish-language ballots. While voters in precincts with populations over 20 percent Hispanic cast one-third of the ballots in the county on November 7, more than half the county's mismarked ballots came from those areas—generally Gore strongholds. "If [the county had used] a Spanish-language ballot, it might very well have cut this problem down quite a bit," argues Timothy Shanahan, director of the Center for Literacy at the University of Chicago. "They might not have made the mistake much at all."

So was it all about discarding ballots? Is this just a story of democracy denied to thousands of Florida voters whose intentions went unrecorded on November 7 or thereafter? Not quite. Republicans who battled with all their might to prevent a hand recount that would have revealed many if not all of the discrepancies detailed here did leap to the battlements in defense of so-called overseas voters. The overseas ballots, a substantial number of which were cast by residents of Florida serving on active military duty in foreign lands, were expected to favor Bush. Republican operatives spared no hyperbole in their defense. When it was learned that as many as 1,400 overseas votes might be disqualified due to irregularities, including the same sort of multiple votes that disqualified 111,262 ballots cast by Floridians who voted in their home precincts on Election Day, the rush to the television cameras was on.

"No one who aspires to be commander in chief should seek to unfairly deny the votes of the men and women he seeks to command," Bush campaign spokeswoman Karen Hughes said at a November 18 news conference in Austin, Texas. "The Democrats have launched a statewide effort to throw out as many military ballots as they can," Montana governor Marc Racicot, a Republican, said the same day. Senator John Warner (R-Va.) dispatched a letter to Defense Secretary William Cohen, demanding that he intervene in cases where military ballots were thrown out in Florida.

When all was said and done, the disputed overseas votes did register an advantage for Bush, giving him 1,380 additional votes, as compared with 750 for Gore. Amazingly, it was Gore who suffered the most from disqualifications of overseas ballots. An investigation by the *New York Times,* published seven months after the election, revealed that while they were raising a patriotic outcry for the counting of all military ballots, Bush aides had secretly devised an elaborate plan for disqualifying military ballots in Democratic counties. The Bush strategy, as detailed in extensive memorandums from the campaign's political and legal teams, was to demand the counting of overseas ballots marked for Bush while pressuring local officials to disqualify ballots marked for Gore. And it worked: Counties carried by Gore ended up accepting only about 20 percent of questionable overseas ballots, while counties carried by Bush accepted roughly 60 percent of the dubious ballots. Judge Anne Kaylor, who chaired the canvassing board in

> ## "In this age of the microchip, we should not have Stone Age voting machines."
>
> —U.S. representative JOHN CONYERS (D-Mich.)

UNDISPUTED in the recent media recounts of the Florida ballots is that thousands of Florida voters went to the polls to cast a vote for president and that vote was not counted.

It was different in Detroit.

What Detroit did was simple. They educated voters. They replaced antiquated punch-card machines with machines that let voters know when the voter made a mistake and gave a voter the opportunity to fix it.

I benefited from these new voting machines. My ballot was kicked out by the machine because I overvoted in a judicial race. If not for this machine, my vote for president, Senate, and Congress might not have been counted. But, because the machine let me know I made a mistake, I got the chance to correct it.

I believe it is inexcusable that this technology is not in every precinct in this country. In the age of the microchip, we shouldn't have Stone Age voting machines.

That is why I have introduced the Equal Protection of Voting Rights Act. It proposes a number of commonsense election reforms. Among these is a uniform baseline standard for voting machines that every voting machine in the United States would be required to meet by 2004. Consistent with what the U.S. Supreme Court held in *Bush* v. *Gore,* Title I of the bill would require states to adopt uniform and nondiscriminatory statewide standards for election machinery. This requirement will not only belatedly *(continued)* end the outdated use of punch-card balloting, but will ensure that states use a consistently optimal level of technology that will protect voters from being disenfranchised by faulty machinery. Too often, minority and poor communities get the worst voting machinery, and too often that means more disenfranchisement in those communities.

In addition, Title I of the legislation requires that states in federal elections allow "provisional voting"—something already used with great success in many states to prevent the exclusion of voters who can later show they were properly registered and improperly denied the opportunity to vote. This would help address the problem of wrongful purges and improper voter intimidation at the polling places—something that African Americans are all too familiar with in our voting experience in this country.

The bill fully funds the implementation of these standards and, therefore, avoids creating an unfunded federal mandate.

Under the Equal Protection of Voting Rights Act, every voting machine would be required to notify voters of overvotes and undervotes. This is a simple, commonsense solution that would make a world of difference.

John Conyers is the ranking Democrat on the House Judiciary Committee and the dean of the Congressional Black Caucus. In April 2001, after the first 100 days of the Bush presidency had passed without action on election reform, he said, "For a president who promised to unite the nation to fail to heal the election's wounds that still divide us is a failure of leadership, and he needs to be held accountable for this failure." To remind the public of Bush's inaction on this issue, he arranged for the web site of Democrats in the Judiciary Committee to carry a rolling ticker that displays the number of days Bush has failed to lead on election reform. (The Judiciary Democrats web site is www.house.gov/judiciary_democrats/demhome.htm.)

Florida's Polk County, makes the case that Republican pressure caused bad ballots to be counted. "I think the rules were bent," the judge argues. "Technically, [at least some of the ballots that were counted] were not supposed to be accepted. Any canvassing board that says they weren't under pressure is being less than candid."

In all, the *Times* found that at least 680 ballots that failed to meet standards for inclusion in the count were recorded as valid votes. More than half of the questionable ballots that were counted had no evidence that they were cast before or on Election Day—as required by law. Other ballots featured no overseas postmark, lacked required signatures, came from voters who were not registered in Florida, or cast two votes for president. In at least 19 cases of "overvoting" by overseas electors, both votes were counted. Had this standard—which Bush aides insisted be used for military ballots—been applied to all ballots cast by Floridians, Gore would have picked up 84,197 votes to 37,731 for Bush. Adjusting for the 537-vote lead awarded Bush by Katherine Harris, the new count based on the Republican standard would have yielded a 45,929 vote win for Gore.

Of course, the liberal standard was applied only where it was likely to aid Bush. Thus, in Miami-Dade, a Democratic-leaning county, almost half of the 307 overseas absentee ballots were thrown out due to objections raised by Republican observers. The Republican tactic of demanding that military votes be counted and then quietly forcing the rejection of military votes they didn't like worked brilliantly. Bush piled up hundreds of needed votes while confused and intimidated Democrats retreated from the battle lines. Though they could have pushed their objections to many of the overseas votes registered for Bush, battered Gore campaign aides went silent regarding questionable votes. After having been called everything short of traitors for attempting to apply the same legal requirements to overseas ballots as

One Republican standard, if applied statewide, would have yielded a 42,929 vote advantage for Gore

those used for ballots cast at home, Democrats folded their tent in the great overseas-ballot fight.

The Bush campaign's manipulation of the overseas-ballot count was just one example of the behind-the-scenes maneuvering that cost Gore Florida. While the overseas-ballot fight at least garnered attention when it was going on, one of the most elaborate Republican scams was unknown to anyone outside the party's inner circle until long after the conclusion of the 36-day tussle over how to count Florida's disputed ballots.

What Gore's lawyers—and most, if not all, of the media—did not know was that poll workers across the state had quietly made a dramatic contribution to Bush's total vote. Only in May 2001 did Florida newspapers reveal that, on Election Day, election officials from 26 Florida counties had "re-created" more than 10,000 absentee ballots that had been mangled in the mail and sorting process and thus could not be read by vote-scanning equipment. So cloaked in mystery had the vote re-creation scheme been that, when Kendall Coffey, one of the chief lawyers for Gore's recount team, learned of it, he said in May, "I never heard this was going on until now." Coffey called the news "startling." In the whole Florida fight, this was a rare example of understatement.

Under no scrutiny from the media or Democratic, Republican, or nonpartisan election observers, officials determined the "clear intent" of voters who had cast the torn or shredded absentee ballots and then filled out new ballots, which were then run through the scanning machines—registering the votes marked by the poll workers.

This would seem to be precisely the sort of intervention that the Bush campaign opposed when it so loudly objected to the full hand-recount of disputed Florida ballots that Gore backers sought. After limited hand recounts in Palm Beach, Broward, and Miami-Dade

FORMER PRESIDENT JIMMY CARTER:

// This past year, the Carter Center monitored six elections in the world. Three were in Latin America, and the others were in Asia and Africa. But we have certain minimal standards in a country before we will go in there at all. And we would not dream of going into a country that had election laws like ours, where there is such a vast chasm in some central nonpartisan or bipartisan agency deciding on election arguments. And also, where every precinct, every voting place, can have a separate kind of voting mechanism, and where the interpretation of what is a good vote or a bad vote depends, almost exclusively, on local officials' prejudices. So we require uniformity in the type of voting and in the standardization of what is a good vote, and we also require that a central election commission be available, on a nonpartisan basis, in order to make judgments during a contest period immediately before, during, or after an election. **//**

Counties were completed in November, Bush himself said, "As Americans have watched on television, they have seen for themselves that manual counting, with individuals making subjective decisions about voter intent, introduces human error and politics into the vote-counting process. Each time these voting cards are handled, the potential for errors multiplies. Additional manual counts of votes that have been counted and recounted will make the process less accurate, not more so."

*   *   *

Yet, neither Bush nor any other prominent Republican has objected to the extraordinary measures to which election officials went to "re-create" mangled absentee ballots. Why so? Perhaps because the Florida Republican Party had poured hundreds of thousands of dollars into a campaign to up the number of absentee votes for George Bush—a campaign that featured personal appeals from Florida governor Jeb Bush and other party bigs. The campaign paid off, as Bush prevailed among voters casting absentee ballots by an almost 2 to 1 margin. Thus, if the re-created ballots were cast by typical absentee voters, the extra help from local election officials in those 26 counties yielded the Republican nominee at least 3,300 crucial votes.

For a candidate whose official margin of victory was barely 500 votes, that's nothing to complain about.

And, so far, neither George W. Bush nor any other Republican has.

What do all the details of flawed voting systems, bad ballot designs, and human errors add up to? If you're George W. Bush, nothing less than the key to the Oval Office.

If you're Al Gore's chief legal strategist in Florida, Ron Klain, they add up to the cold comfort of knowing that what you said all along was true: "There is no question that the majority of people on Election Day believed they left the booth voting for Al Gore."

And if you are one of the more than 170,000 Florida voters whose ballots were not counted in what may well have been the most significant election of your lifetime, it adds up to a lot of right-wing commentators calling you "stupid" because the people who get paid to put on elections failed—miserably.

CHAPTER 4

Jews for Buchanan:

A Palm Beach Story

This is how Pat Buchanan, the Reform Party nominee
for president in 2000, explains the "Jews-for-Buchanan" phenomenon
that earned his candidacy its greatest attention:

"In October of 2000, as the election got closer, it was clear that
things weren't working out for our presidential campaign. We had had
a good Reform Party convention, but after that we just couldn't seem
to get off the ground. We put some television and radio ads up in
some states, and we had some fine people working for us. But when
the debates were closed to us, that was it. Worse, the race between
Gore and Bush was close; neither of them was opening a lead—which
meant that even some voters who might have been inclined to cast a
protest vote for me were going to be afraid to waste it."

After one particularly long day of campaigning, Buchanan says, he
was drifting off to sleep when it occurred to him that the race between
Gore and Bush was so close that even the small percentage of ballots

*"These
aren't
my
votes"*

cast for him could exceed the margin separating the Democratic and Republican nominees in the battleground states that would decide the election. The thought, he says, horrified him. "I was in the Bush caucus of the Buchanan campaign. Some people working with me thought, 'Well, if we can't win, let's make things as bad as can be and give it to Gore.' But that's not where I was at. I wanted to get a good vote; I wasn't going to vote for Bush. But if it was going to be Bush or Gore, I definitely wanted George W. Bush to be the one taking the oath of office on January 20."

So Buchanan, former aide to Presidents Nixon and Reagan, bombastic CNN commentator, and righteously indignant challenger of the political status quo, put his palms together and prayed. "I said, 'God, please don't let it turn out, when I'm dead and gone, that my gravestone reads *Pat Buchanan: The Man Who Cost George W. Bush the Presidency.* Please, don't let that be my epitaph.'"

The next night, Buchanan says, he made the same request of the Almighty. After several nights of this, he heard a disembodied voice speaking to him. "Pat," said God, "I've always liked you. So here's what I'm going to do: I'm going to make sure that your votes don't prevent George W. Bush from becoming president. In fact, I'll go you one better. I'm going to make sure that your votes are the ones that cost Al Gore the presidency. And to guarantee that there is no confusion about this, I'm going to use my chosen people to close the deal. I'm going to get the Jews of Florida to vote for you—not a few, but thousands of them, coming from their condos and retirement centers to place a mark by Pat Buchanan's name."

Buchanan says he took it all in, amazed that his beleaguered candidacy would be saved the final embarrassment by Divine Intervention. Then, he heard the voice anew. "One more thing, Pat," began the King of Kings, "I will do all of this for you. I will turn the tide of history for you. But, Pat, you gotta cut this crap out. I'm tired of having to bail out your losing campaigns."

A wry grin crosses the visage that is so familiar to viewers of television public affairs programs. Soon, he is laughing out loud—the Irish storyteller delighting in his capacity to spin a yarn.

When he has had his laugh, Buchanan finally turns serious. "That," he says, "is about as likely a story as the one that says all those elderly Jewish Democrats in Palm Beach County actually intended to vote for me."

Pat Buchanan does not accept the charge that he is an anti-Semite. It's true that he thinks Israel wields too much influence over U.S. policy in the Middle East, and, yes, Buchanan has questioned the wisdom of tracking down and prosecuting elderly eastern Europeans who worked as guards in concentration camps, and, well, yes, he was the adviser who told then-president Ronald Reagan to visit the German military cemetery at Bitburg, where member's of Hitler's SS are buried. But, Buchanan notes, some of the most loyal supporters of his three presidential campaigns were Jews. "In fact, the guy who fought the hardest to get us on the ballot in Florida last year was a Jewish fellow," Buchanan recalled in the first interview he had given on the subject since the week of confusion and retribution that followed Florida's fiasco of November 7. Buchanan searched his memory. "Yes, David Goldman, great guy. He worked very hard for us down there."

While Buchanan delights in ticking off the names of his Jewish aides and allies, however, he recognizes that they are the exceptions to the rules of American politics. And he is aware of the ironic implications of his unexpected—and unlikely—appeal among from the Children of Israel.

Buchanan knows that he is not a beloved figure among the retired garment workers, former New York social service employees, and

"In fact, the guy who fought the hardest to get us on the ballot in Florida last year was a Jewish fellow"

—PAT BUCHANAN

Holocaust survivors who make up such a sizable portion of Palm Beach County's electorate. "Look, I am not unaware of what 20 years of accusations in the media can do to your reputation. Remember, I worked for Richard Nixon. I heard one old fellow in Palm Beach County say he would sooner vote for Farrakhan than Pat Buchanan," he says. "And even if they didn't have anything against me, I'm not sure how many people in Palm Beach were aware we were running. We didn't do much campaigning down there. If they relied on the debates or the network news for information about our candidacy, most of them probably didn't even know that Pat Buchanan was running for president in 2000."

So how did Buchanan end up winning one of his best vote totals in all the nation from the overwhelmingly Democratic, heavily Jewish and Haitian-American county? "C'mon," he drawls, "It was the butterfly ballot. Everyone knows that now."

On November 7, however, "butterfly ballots" were no more a part of the political language than "hanging chads." Certainly, Pat Buchanan wasn't thinking about ballot-design issues that day. Instead, he was trying to close off the least successful of his three presidential campaigns with a measure of dignity. Buchanan is as loyal to his small band of followers as they are to him, and even if he was about to experience some serious political humiliation, he was not about to let his "Buchanan Brigades" down. The campaign rented a hotel ballroom in suburban Virginia, laid in a supply of chips and beer, and prepared for a long night of disappointment. There were a few bright spots. "I think we did a little better than expected in Maine and North Dakota," Buchanan recalls. But as the night wore on, it became painfully evident that the Reform Party vote nationwide would fall far short of the 5 percent needed to maintain the federal funding Ross Perot had secured with his ego-trip candidacies of 1992 and 1996. When all the votes were count-

"It was the butterfly ballot. Everyone knows that now"

—PAT BUCHANAN

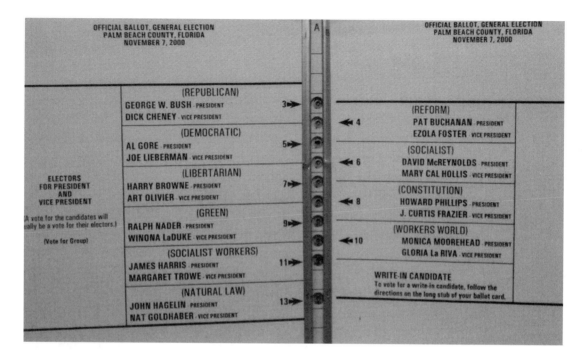

ed, in fact, it would turn out that Buchanan's Reform Party campaign had not even won one-half of 1 percent of the vote, making the third party's collapse one of the most dramatic in American history.

Buchanan recalls noticing on election night that he had done a good deal better in Florida than in other states, and he heard talk of ballot confusion in south Florida—even catching a reference on television to Palm Beach County's controversial butterfly ballot. But mostly he was just thinking about getting home to his stately manor off a tree-lined country road a few miles from the Potomac River. He gave a concession speech and then left to watch the seesawing contest between Gore and Bush. Early in the morning, after most of the networks had called

Florida for the Republican, he and his wife finally went to bed—putting a depressing campaign and any fears that his candidacy might have cost Bush the presidency behind them.

When Buchanan awoke around 7:00 A.M., he found his political world turned upside down. Embarrassed television networks—many of which he had worked for at one time or another—had retracted their declarations for Bush. Neither candidate had yet secured the needed 270 electoral votes; Florida, the state that would decide the contest, was "too close to call." Legal teams were being mobilized, Gore and Bush were in seclusion, and the fourth candidate of the 2000 race suddenly found himself an excited spectator. "I'm enough of a historian and a political junkie to know this doesn't happen more than once or twice in a lifetime so, of course, I was fascinated. Like everyone else, I was watching to see what came next," Buchanan recalls. "But, as I flipped around the channels, it was strange. I kept seeing my picture pop up. I said to my wife, 'You know, they're talking about our campaign more after the election than they did all fall.' I honestly didn't know why at first. But then I started hearing the reports from Palm Beach County, the reports about the butterfly ballot. There were people crying, yelling, saying they had been confused. And when I saw the ballot, I understood why."

The butterfly ballot that caused so much confusion in Palm Beach County looked as bizarre to Buchanan as it did to everyone else who was waking up to its reality on the morning of November 8. "They had names of the candidates along both sides, and you voted in the middle—which seemed a little strange. And the spaces you were supposed to mark if you wanted to vote for a particular candidate weren't aligned with the candidate's name," he remembers thinking. "It was obviously confusing. I think I could have been confused by it—especially when there was a high-turnout election and all this pressure to vote quickly."

"There were people crying, yelling, saying they had been confused"

—PAT BUCHANAN

Buchanan had no doubt that mistakes had been made in Palm Beach County. He knew the region's ethnic and political mix—he and his wife have a condo in Delray Beach. Twenty-five percent of the county's 1,050,000 residents are Jewish, another 25 percent are African American and Latino, and even in the most lopsided Republican landslides, Palm Beach County remains reliably Democratic—even with the ballot confusion, Gore beat Bush in the county by a staggering 26 percent margin in 2000. Indeed, if Palm Beach County is known for anything in Florida politics, it is its liberalism. The county sends the legislature's most reliably liberal members, such as State House Minority Leader Lois Frankel, to Tallahassee.

In other words, the candidate was well aware that Palm Beach was as far from Buchanan country as you could get. He also knew that, with fewer than 1,000 votes separating Bush and Gore in Florida, and with roughly 3,000 potential Gore votes registered for Buchanan in Palm Beach County, those votes for him might well have changed the course of American political history. And if there had been any question in his mind, all Buchanan had to do was watch the television reports of the people from Jewish retirement communities up and down Palm Beach County. Retiree Shirley Datz, a resident of the Lakes of Delray retirement community, summed things up when asked if there was any chance that the 47 votes Buchanan received there were reflective of the sentiments of her neighbors. "Impossible," Datz exclaimed. "Even one vote for Buchanan would be impossible here."

Finally, Buchanan called his sister, Bay, his most trusted adviser. "I remember saying to Bay, 'Look, we really should say something. These aren't my votes.'" Bay Buchanan agreed. A veteran campaigner who had run for state treasurer of California and essentially managed her brother's three presidential campaigns, she saw a passel of problems in Palm Beach. Among them the following:

> "Even one vote for Buchanan would be impossible here"
>
> —SHIRLEY DATZ, PALM BEACH COUNTY VOTER

☞ Buchanan's percentage of the vote in Palm Beach County was dramatically higher than the percentage of the vote he received statewide. In fact, it was dramatically higher than the vote he got in his strongholds in Florida and nationally.

☞ Buchanan received 20 percent of the votes he got in the entire state of Florida from Palm Beach County alone. In the 1996 Republican presidential primary campaign, when he was a much stronger contender, Buchanan got just 5 percent of his statewide vote from the county.

☞ Palm Beach County had actually been a center of opposition to Buchanan within Florida Reform Party circles. As Reform Party leader David Goldman admitted, "That Buchanan got that many votes in Palm Beach County is prima facie evidence of a terrible mistake transpiring. If Palm Beach County is a Buchanan stronghold, then so is my local synagogue."

☞ Buchanan's fall campaign had never gotten traction even in Florida counties where it was expected to show strength. In Tampa and the north Florida Panhandle, where Buchanan campaigned and broadcast commercials, Bay noted, Pat collected only about 1,000 to 1,200 votes—far less than Palm Beach County's 3,407, where Buchanan did not campaign and bought no advertising.

"This is not the time to spin. It is too important," said Bay Buchanan. So she and her brother reviewed the pile of interview requests that had poured in. They decided to go with NBC's *Today* show. Before Buchanan settled into his chair the next morning, Palm Beach County had boiled over. There were near riots in the streets, police were separating Gore and Bush backers. Jewish retirees and Jesse Jackson were putting old differences behind them to call for a new vote. And everyone was talking about the Buchanan ballots.

"It was really spinning out of control," Buchanan says. "I didn't know if what I had to say was going to change anything. But I thought it might clarify something. I wanted to explain that, 'Hey, I wish those were my votes. I really do. But they're not.'"

Indeed, Buchanan figures that, of the 3,407 votes he received in Palm Beach County, only around 300 to 400 came from his supporters. That's a figure that fits with the numbers cited by Jim Cunningham, chair of the executive committee of Palm Beach County's Reform Party, regarding the size of the local Buchanan Brigade. "The rest, I'm quite sure, were Gore votes," says Buchanan, echoing what he told the national television audience on the morning of November 8.

In a sea of postelection spin, Buchanan's frankness was an island of honest comment. And it had a dramatic impact. Democrats delighted in Buchanan's comments. Republicans were furious that their "spin" had been undone. Bush campaign spokesman Ari Fleischer, seeking to avert calls for a new vote, told reporters that the region was, in fact, "a Buchanan stronghold in Florida." Political strategist Karl Rove—the man Texans call "Bush's brain"—was busily pulling aside reporters for private briefings on how Palm Beach County was indeed Buchanan Country. It was a laughable exercise, except that—in a tense and confusing moment—the Bush people were gambling that it just might work.

The Bush campaign had its media mouthpieces, talk radio's Rush Limbaugh and Fox Television, spinning their line. Limbaugh, who owns a Palm Beach mansion, pronounced the ballot perfectly readable and dismissed the controversy as a tempest in the ideological teapot. "Liberals assume all the votes are theirs, that's how they play the game," he said. "Liberals are more cutthroat than they've ever been."

> "Hey, I wish those were my votes. I really do. But they're not"
>
> —Pat Buchanan

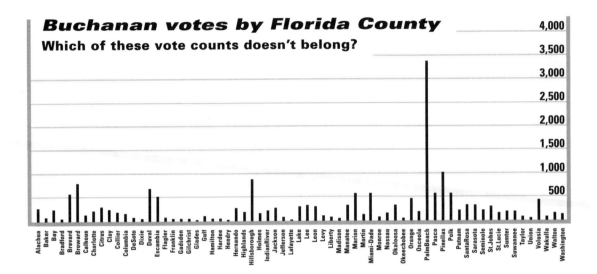

Buchanan votes by Florida County

Which of these vote counts doesn't belong?

Never mind that one of the biggest names in American conservatism was joining the chorus of complaint about the butterfly ballot. If Buchanan wasn't on board, the spin went, then he was guilty of aiding and abetting the enemy.

When Buchanan agreed to appear on a Fox program after the *Today* show appearance, he was hit with both barrels. "The fellow who was interviewing me was someone I knew. I'd been on with him before, but this time he was very serious. He asked, 'Why do you hate the Bushes so much that you would do this to them?'" Buchanan recalls. "I said, 'Look, I don't hate the Bushes. I hope George W. Bush wins.'"

Over the next several days, Buchanan began to get calls from old friends and key players in the Republican Party, who were saying things like, "You've got to say those Palm Beach votes were yours," or asking "How can you do this to George W. Bush?" Finally, Buchanan decided to get out of the crossfire. He withdrew to the basement of his

Virginia home and began writing a book that will appear later this year—on the decline of Western civilization.

"I watched the rest of the Florida thing play out on television—without me," he says. "I chose not to insert myself into it anymore. It had all become so intense, so bitter, that it didn't seem as if people were interested in talking about what had obviously happened in Palm Beach County and the rest of Florida."

Bush was sworn in as president. And, as spring turned to summer, Buchanan followed the media recounts from the book-lined study of his home—where a gold-plated pitchfork, the symbol of his presidential campaigns, stands by one wall, and huge pictures of Buchanan with Nixon and Reagan occupy a side hallway. Even the most generous recounts in Bush's favor—particularly that of Florida secretary of state Katherine Harris—continued to show that the votes Buchanan took from the Democrat's column in Palm Beach County would have been more than enough to place Gore in the White House. There were also roughly 10,000 uncounted "overvotes" from counties across Florida that were rejected because they were marked for both Buchanan and Gore. "I would say 95 to 98 percent of them were for Gore," says Buchanan. "They came from precincts that voted for Gore."

Buchanan worries that the whole mess in Florida will feed a creeping political cynicism that already has undermined democratic institutions. But, yes, he is still amused by the whole "Jews-for-Buchanan" thing. Told that precinct-by-precinct analyses of Palm Beach County found that, in addition to elderly Jews, Haitian-American immigrants also cast disproportionately high numbers of votes for him, Buchanan laughed. A frequent and fierce critic of liberal immigration policies, he said, "Who would have guessed that the story of the 2000 election would be that Pat Buchanan is the candidate of Jews and immigrants?"

"I don't think there's any question that more Gore votes were lost in the process than Bush votes"

—PAT BUCHANAN

But the final analysis of what happened in Florida is less ironic—and far more troubling for a nation where elections are supposed to reflect the will of the people. Buchanan's bottom line: "When you look at all the numbers from Florida, all the reports of butterfly ballots, of undervotes and overvotes, and when you look at where they came from, I don't think there's any question that more Gore votes were lost in the process than Bush votes." What does this mean? "That more Gore voters went to the polls than Bush voters on November 7 in Florida," says Pat Buchanan. "If the results had reflected the actual sentiments of the people who voted, Al Gore would have won Florida, which means he would have had the majority in the electoral college and that he would be president today."

Buchanan is quiet for a moment. "I suppose I'll get it from my conservative friends for saying that, but I don't have to spin it, do I? I mean, I haven't gotten a thank-you call from George W. Bush. Besides, I think there's a certain duty to try to keep the historical record straight, even if it doesn't change the fact of who is in the White House."

Speaking of history, there is one souvenir from the 2000 campaign that Buchanan says he still has to get his hands on. "I've got to write to Theresa LePore down there in Palm Beach County and ask her for one of those butterfly ballots," he says, smiling once more. "The design of that ballot probably got me more votes than anything I did or said during the 2000 campaign."

Suddenly Socialist—
Palm Beach County's Radical Ballot

A few days after the November 7 election, one of the subtler ripples of the media splash that followed the Florida fiasco hit the cramped Manhattan headquarters of the Socialist Party USA. The phone that

OVERVOTING FOR GORE

Palm Beach County's butterfly ballot placed the names of candidates for president in two separate columns. Experts on ballot design say this is one of the worst sins in ballot layout, since dividing the names of candidates for the same office in this way encourages well-meaning citizens to cast votes for one candidate in each column. This is called an overvote, and the ballot is discarded. The butterfly ballot produced almost 20,000 overvote ballots in Palm Beach County—disqualifying every one.

Here are the overvote figures:

☞ Palm Beach County overvotes on the presidential ballot where ten candidate names were listed across two columns: 19,125.

☞ Palm Beach County overvotes on the U.S. Senate ballot where seven candidate names were listed in a single column: 1,530.

☞ Palm Beach County overvotes in 1996 when candidate names were listed in one column: less than 1 per 100.

☞ Palm Beach County overvotes in 2000 when candidate names were listed in two columns: 4.2 per 100.

☞ Number of Palm Beach County overvote ballots on which one of the votes was for Al Gore: 15,371.

☞ Number of Palm Beach County overvote ballots on which one of the votes was for George W. Bush: 3,751.

☞ Percent of overvote ballots that included a vote for Al Gore: 80.

☞ Percent of overvote ballots that included a vote for George W. Bush: 19.5.

☞ Overvotes for Democrat Al Gore and Reform candidate Pat Buchanan: 5,330.

☞ Gore-Buchanan overvoters who voted Democrat for U.S. Senate: 4,425 (83 percent).

(continued)

☞ "You get a pretty clear pattern from these ballots. Most of these people went to the polls to vote for Gore."

—Anthony Salvanto, University of California–Irvine expert in voting patterns

☞ "These [Palm Beach County voters] are people who knew how to vote. Typically, they do it right. But the butterfly ballot discombobulated them. Are these stupid voters? Or is it a stupid voting system? There's certainly evidence that these were not stupid voters."

—Henry Brady, University of California–Berkeley specialist in voting behavior

☞ "Hindsight is 20-20. But I'll never do it again."

—Theresa LePore, Palm Beach County supervisor of elections

☞ "It's got to be on one page."

—Pam Iorio, President, Florida State Association of Supervisors of Elections.

Florida's election laws specify that, in order to avoid confusion, the place for marking votes should be to the right of a candidate's name. On the butterfly ballot, however, the places for voting for Pat Buchanan and David McReynolds—the two third-party candidates who got the most overvotes, and the most disproportionately high vote in Palm Beach County—were to the left of their names. The bottom line? "It was an illegal ballot," says Representative Irv Slosberg, who represents Palm Beach County in the Florida legislature. As a result, adds Slosberg, "We had 20,000 people disenfranchised here."

rarely rang during an election campaign in which party candidate David McReynolds struggled to garner a six-word mention in the *New York Times* was suddenly rattling off the hook.

What, the mandarins of multinational media wanted to know, did Socialists think about the prospect that they might be responsible for handing the presidency to George W. Bush? The small band of radicals, heirs to the legacy of the presidential candidacies of Eugene Victor Debs and Norman Thomas, quickly devised a high-tech response. They changed the outgoing message on the party's phone line to say: "You have reached the Socialist Party campaign office, where our motto is, 'It's not our fault that Al Gore lost Florida.'"

That message was probably right. It is true that the 622 votes McReynolds received in Florida added up to 85 more than the 537-vote margin of victory Katherine Harris and Jeb Bush certified for George W. But it is also true that McReynolds, an articulate gay pacifist with a history of activism as a leader of the War Resisters League, had enough appeal to garner his share of votes—especially in south Florida, where there are still a few elderly garment workers who remember when the Socialist Party provided most of the New Deal's best ideas.

So why was McReynolds suddenly such a hot topic? Because, while McReynolds certainly earned his share of votes in Palm Beach County, no one, not even the candidate himself, claims that all of the votes he received from the waterfront towns of Florida's east coast came from Socialists—or from fellow travelers.

Even accounting for the vagaries of left-wing nostalgia, McReynolds got way more than his piece of the Palm Beach County vote. In fact, of his 622 votes in all of Florida, 302 came from Palm Beach County alone. Of Florida's 67 counties, 53 gave McReynolds 5 votes or fewer. None gave him more than 35 votes, save for Palm Beach.

Either Palm Beach County is the weirdest piece of political real estate on the planet—an overwhelmingly Democratic region with a penchant for Pat Buchanan and openly gay Socialists—or there was something seriously wrong with the ballot. For his part, McReynolds was smart enough—and graceful enough—to acknowledge that his political fortunes were aided by a bad ballot.

On Theresa LePore's infamous "butterfly ballot" McReynolds was listed—ironically—on the right wing, directly beneath the Reform Party's Buchanan.

While the bulk of the mispunched votes went to Buchanan, whose oval was the first of those next to Gore's name, the disproportionate Palm Beach County vote for a thoughtful democratic Socialist was, if anything, even more disconcerting. While Palm Beach County provided Buchanan with almost 1 percent of his total national vote, it delivered McReynolds more than 3 percent of his national total.

The McReynolds vote is not merely a bizarre footnote to the Florida fiasco. It really should tip the balance in any debate over whether a structural flaw cost Al Gore the votes he needed to win Florida. Consider the following:

☞ No other county in the state of Florida used a butterfly ballot on November 7. Indeed, Jay Bennett, director of elections for Fidlar Doubleday, one of the nation's largest manufacturers of punch-card ballots, told the Fort Lauderdale *Sun-Sentinel* that he had never seen a butterfly ballot used in a presidential election. "It has been used in [referendum and judicial retention] elections where there is a lot of text, but I've not seen it in the candidate format."

☞ It has been claimed that LePore had to adopt the butterfly ballot because of the large number of presidential candidates—10—who qualified in Florida. But, the states of Washington and Colorado also had 10 candidates on their ballots and those states reported no problem listing candidates in one column. Veteran election officials in other states say LePore violated rule number 1 of ballot design: Never split names into two columns. "That's just something experience has taught us you don't do," says John Pearson, Washington's senior assistant director for elections. "You don't even split them by page or by column because you are inviting overvotes when you do that."

☞ Even LePore, who maintains she designed the ballot to benefit nearsighted elderly voters, admits that her design created an electoral nightmare. "I'll never use facing pages like that [again]," she now says.

Did the Palm Beach ballot debacle cost Al Gore the presidency? While other counties had screwups that cost Gore dearly, none can be said to have so dramatically damaged his presidential prospects. There were two distinct ways in which LePore's ballot diverted votes that would have padded the Democratic margin in Palm Beach County, shifted the statewide result, and made Al Gore president:

☞ First, thousands of voters who went to the polls to elect Gore unintentionally cast their ballots for Buchanan and McReynolds. The voters themselves have acknowledged as much: "I made the mistake," Siggy Flicker, a 33-year-old Gore backer from Boca Raton, told the local paper. Gore lost, says Flicker, "because of people like me." A consortium of statisticians and political scientists from Harvard, Cornell, and Northwestern who reviewed the Palm Beach County results shared Flicker's view, as did other statisticians from major universities across the country. As Greg D. Adams, an assistant professor in the Department of Social and Decision Sciences at Carnegie Mellon

"I'll never use facing pages like that [again]," Theresa LePore now says

University, explains, "It can be claimed with a high degree of statistical confidence that the mistakes (in Palm Beach County) cost Gore somewhere between 2,000 and 3,000 votes." How much statistical confidence? "Greater than 99.99999 [percent]," says Chris Carroll, an associate professor of economics at Johns Hopkins University who specializes in statistical analysis. Considering the statewide pattern of voting, adds Craig R. Fox, an associate professor of management at Duke University, the probability of so high a vote for Buchanan and McReynolds in Palm Beach County "is less than 1 in 10,000, which is approximately equivalent to the odds that you will be injured by your toilet bowl cleaner this year."

☞ Second, LePore's confusing design led to the spoiling of 19,120 Palm Beach County ballots on which more than one vote was cast for president. The rate of overvoting was 4.1 percent—meaning that more than 4 out of every 100 ballots cast in the county were tossed because people cast two votes for president. By comparison, in Leon County, Florida, the rate of double voting was less than .20 ballots per 100. It is not even necessary to look beyond the borders of Palm Beach County to find evidence of how LePore's flawed ballot altered the presidential election result. In other November 7 races where Palm Beach County voters were not forced to use butterfly ballots, the overvoting rate was dramatically lower—a mere .13 percent in the races for state insurance commissioner and state education commissioner, and just .83 in the multicandidate race for U.S. Senate. How many votes did Gore lose because of overvotes? the *Palm Beach Post* conducted a ballot-by-ballot review, and concluded, "Confusion over Palm Beach County's butterfly ballot cost Al Gore about 6,600 votes, more than 10 times what he needed to overcome George W. Bush's slim lead in Florida and win the presidency." Here's

Gore lost, says Flicker, "because of people like me"

The McReynolds Vote in Florida, 2000

Palm Beach

Alachua Baker
Bay Bradford Brevard
Broward Calhoun
Charlotte Citrus Clay Collier
Columbia DeSoto Dixie Duval
Escambia Flagler Franklin
Gadsden Gilchrist Glades Gulf
Hamilton Hardee Hendry Hernando
Highlands Hillsborough Holmes
Indian River Jackson Jefferson
Lafayette Lake Lee Leon Levy
Liberty Madison Manatee Marion
Martin Miami-Dade Monroe
Nassau Okaloosa Okeechobee
Orange Osceola Pasco Pinellas
Polk Putnam Santa Rosa
Sarasota Seminole St. Johns
St. Lucie Sumter Suwannee
Taylor Union Volusia
Wakulla Walton
Washington

Palm Beach County was responsible for almost half of the votes cast for McReynolds in the state of Florida. In 53 of the 66 other counties, he earned 5 or fewer votes.

Palm Beach County gave McReynolds more than 3 percent of his national total.

what the *Post* found: 5,330 Palm Beach County residents cast votes for Gore and Buchanan and 2,908 cast votes for Gore and McReynolds. Subtract 1,631 overvotes for Bush and Buchanan, and you get an advantage of 6,607 votes for Gore. Even allowing that each third-party candidate may actually have deserved 1 percent of these overvotes, that still leaves Gore with a 6,500 vote increase in his Palm Beach County total.

Combine this conservative estimate of the number of votes Gore lost to spoiled ballots with a conservative estimate of the number of unintended votes for Buchanan or McReynolds and the figure goes even higher: To the point where it can be argued that a startling 8,500 votes were lost for Gore because of ballot-design flaws.

Perhaps it is best to turn, for the last word, to a man who knows a thing or two about the voting in Palm Beach County—but who dismissed both Al Gore and George W. Bush as capitalist tools.

"Yes, the election was extremely close. Yes, had Gore won a few more votes in another couple of states, the issues in Florida would not be important. And, yes, Gore did win the popular vote and thus gives new impetus to abolishing the electoral college. But the fact is, this election came down to the state of Florida, and whatever Gore's motives in pursuing this to the bitter end, the nation owes him a debt of thanks for having caused us to focus on the Florida balloting," says David McReynolds. "For a nation that lectures on how elections should be conducted, we saw an election stolen by George W. Bush and the Republican Party. One does not have to support Al Gore to recognize a theft in broad daylight."

No Remedy
The Rough Justice That Denied Democracy

"Some circuit judge in Palm Beach County will decide the fate of the country."

—University of Florida political science professor Richard Sher

"Florida Judge Denies New Voting in Palm Beach County."

—Headline, November 20, 2000

On the morning of November 8, 2000, as most Americans were only beginning to comprehend the scope of the mess in Florida, Senator Bob Kerrey (D-Nebr.) was already offering a solution. The whole state, said Kerrey, should simply vote again.

"I'm still hopeful that Gore wins, but the fairest thing to do in Florida right now if they find continued irregularities [is to] organize and schedule a runoff election just for Florida," Kerrey told reporters.

Kerrey was proposing a do over. And he was not alone.

Two days later, Harvard law professor Philip B. Heymann argued that, because the butterfly form used in Palm Beach County clearly violated Florida statutes designed to avoid confusion over where to mark a vote by specifying the structure of ballots, state officials should forget about recounts and other "solutions" that would necessarily rely upon discredited ballots. Instead, the former deputy attorney general of the United States said, "The other and better path is to quickly order a new vote in Palm Beach County using a ballot in the legally prescribed form."

If the always-too-cautious Gore campaign was hesitating to embrace a do over along the lines proposed by Kerrey or Heymann, the idea certainly was popular with Palm Beach County voters. And it had relevance for voters across the state—tens of thousands of whom were disenfranchised by ill-advised and frequently illegal election practices that skewed the results of the November 7 vote. A stack of lawsuits were filed by dissatisfied and disenfranchised voters, whose lawyers were, within days after the election, asking judges to order some form of revote. In a suit on behalf of Palm Beach Countians Beverly Rogers and Ray Kaplan, one team of lawyers argued: "An election is a vehicle by which a selection of a winning candidate is to be achieved. The will and intent of the people is the primary focus in any election challenge. Where that goal is not achieved in an initial election, courts must have available to them a remedy to achieve a fair outcome. The remedies available must be flexible in order to account for the unforeseeable or unpredictable circumstances not contemplated in the general election laws. In this

"Courts must have available to them a remedy to achieve a fair outcome"

—LEGAL BRIEF SEEKING A REVOTE IN PALM BEACH COUNTY

regard, courts must be vested with a tremendous amount of discretion to effectuate whatever equitable relief is necessary to give voters a further chance, in a fair election, to express their views. Given the foregoing principles and statutory pronouncements, there really can be no good faith dispute that trial courts have the power and ability to order new elections."

The complaining voters had the weight of federal and state law on their side. The U.S. Code governing elections for president clearly authorizes states to resolve "any controversy or contest concerning the appointment of all or any of the [presidential] electors . . . by judicial or other methods or procedures." Federal judge Donald Middlebrooks, in rejecting one of several attempts by the Bush campaign to prevent local and state officials from forging an equitable solution to the disputed election, ruled that "federal law gives states the exclusive power to resolve controversies over the manner in which presidential electors are selected."

Florida statutes were equally blunt. Relying on the time-honored legal maxim that "for every wrong there is a remedy," they stated that a circuit judge ruling on a lawsuit was empowered to "fashion such orders as he or she deems necessary to ensure that each allegation in the complaint is investigated, examined or checked, to prevent or correct any alleged wrong, and to provide any appropriate relief under such circumstances."

There was not much doubt that a wrong had occurred. As Harvard's Philip B. Heymann noted: "An extremely confusing ballot flatly violated the law that Florida enacted to prevent this confusion. In a state where the candidates [were] separated by hundreds of votes, thousands [of voters] in an overwhelmingly Democratic district seem to have been misled by a confusing ballot form used only there—a form that was directly forbidden by a Florida state statute." There was no doubt as to the extreme nature of the damage to democracy that had occurred as a result of the butterfly ballot: A team of five statisticians from top universities across the country had come to Florida to testify that after studying results from 4,481 election jurisdictions around the country they had determined that Palm Beach County's results were the most irregular in the nation.

What to do about an election that was so obviously flawed in execution and result? Florida judges did not need to look far to determine that the option of ordering a new vote fell well within the definition of "appropriate relief." In a 1998 case involving a disputed election in Florida's Volusia County, the state Supreme Court had ruled that, in cases where a failure on the part of local officials to comply with state election laws had created a reasonable doubt as to whether a certified election expresses the will of the voters, judges must void the contested election. This was based on well-established legal precedent in the state. In a definitive 1984 ruling, a previous Supreme Court had ruled that, where actions on the part of officials had created clear concerns about the integrity of the election process "courts must not be reluctant to invalidate those elections to ensure public credibility in the electoral process."

Lawyers for Rogers and Kaplan argued that "if the results of an entire election are to be voided or set aside, there could be only one remedy—a new election." In a number of cases involving contested elections, their briefs recalled, Florida judges had provided that precise remedy. Henry Handler, an attorney for three Palm Beach County voters, argued that it was wrong to think of the requested relief as a new election; rather, they suggested, the court was being asked to schedule another round of voting to "complete" an election where there was

In a number of cases, Florida judges had called for new elections

Palm Beach: The county's results were the most irregular in the nation.

reasonable doubt as to whether the will of the voters had been ascertained.

These arguments, though grounded in legal precedent and democratic intent, were ridiculed by the Bush campaign and its lawyers. "There is only one body, by law, that can decide this, and that is the Florida legislature," Bush hired gun Barry Richard thundered. Richard argued that there was "not a whisper or a suggestion" in federal or state law indicating anything different. He was, of course, wrong. While it was true that federal courts, such as the U.S. Supreme Court that would eventually decide the Florida contest, were essentially barred from intervening in presidential election disputes—a point

Federal Judge Middlebrooks made in his rejection of one Bush appeal—there were more than just whispers that local and state courts could involve themselves. There were shouts from on high. The U.S. Code sections authorizing states to resolve presidential election disputes specifically mention "judicial" remedies, and there were enough legal precedents to fill several shelves in a law library.

Those precedents were so well established as to create one of the great ironies of the 2000 campaign. While conservative legal theorists were dragooned into action to make the case against a revote, a quick review by Alexander Reid and the editors of the *New York University Law Review* found that one of the more thoughtful defenses of judicial intervention to force a revote was penned by one of the political right's legal icons: Ken Starr. "It is unsurprising," Starr wrote in a 1974 law review article, "that the courts have accepted proof of a possible effect on outcome as sufficient to invoke the invalidation remedy. This is a burden which may readily be carried when serious violations occur, and the election is close." Starr wrote that "a new contest is warranted only when illegal acts might skew the election returns sufficiently so as to influence the outcome." But, the conservative legal eagle added, when there is evidence of such a skewed outcome, ordering a revote is "particularly appropriate."

Still, Richard continually claimed that the law gave no indication "that any court—much less a circuit court—has any voice in solving this problem."

Far from being insulted by Richard's "much less a circuit court" dismissal, Palm Beach County Circuit Judge Jorge Labarga seemed to embrace it. Labarga indicated from the moment lawyers entered his West Palm Beach courtroom in mid-November that he was reluctant to exercise the power he had to fix the problem. The case was a daunting one, to be sure—since the ordering of a fair and legal election in Palm

Beach County would almost certainly guarantee the election of Al Gore. That must have been an especially unpleasant prospect for Labarga, a Republican who admitted to lawyers in the case that he had attended GOP rallies and that he might have contributed funds to Republican candidates in recent elections. Labarga said he did not remember exactly how much money he might have given or to which candidates he might have handed checks—although he did add that he was pretty sure he had never had "a one-on-one conversation with Jeb Bush."

One did not have to be a "seasoned legal observer" to determine that Labarga was in no need of instruction from Jeb or other Republican operatives. The Republican judge had the Bush campaign spin down even before Richard made his case. "The voting right is a precious right that I appreciate as deeply as anyone else in this country, but given the constitutional mandate, what authority do I, or any judge, have to order a new election in one county in the nation?" Labarga asked. Apparently relying on spin that had been circulated days earlier by Republican strategists, Labarga suggested that he did not have the authority to order a new vote because Article II, section I, clause 4 of the U.S. Constitution gives Congress sole power to set the date for a presidential election. This "Election Day is sacred" dodge was comic on its face. Elections for federal office now occur mainly on the first Tuesday after the first Monday in November—though Louisiana and Georgia allow runoffs to take place in cases where the leading candidate fails to obtain a majority. But uniformity of voting dates has not been exactly common in federal elections.

Congress did not even settle on the first Tuesday after the first Monday in November as the prescribed date for federal elections until 1845—more than half a century after the country started electing presidents. Prior to that decision, voting took place across an electoral calendar that opened in September and did not close until well into

November. Even after Congress attempted to set a universal date, exceptions were commonly made to the rule. Remember the expression "As Maine goes, so goes the nation"? It was rooted in the fact that, until the election of 1960, Maine voters went to the polls in September. The early vote was permitted in deference to Maine's fierce winters, and Republicans were big fans of the calendar quirk—as Mainers voted for the party's nominee in all but one of the presidential elections during the first 100 years of the GOP's existence.

Even if Judge Labarga chose to hang his hat on the calendar hook, he was in trouble when it came to established constitutional theory regarding the resolution of disputed elections. As Erwin Chemerinsky, a specialist in constitutional law who teaches at the University of California, would explain to the court, "Federal law is clear that it is state law that is to determine any disputes regarding selection of electors." In no way, argued Chemerinsky, should provisions for voting on a particular day be read as a bar on post-election remedies—including revotes—to mitigate against the damage done by illegal actions that thwart the will of the people.

If Chemerinsky's plain language was confusing to Judge Labarga, perhaps the lawyers for the disenfranchised voters of Florida should simply have called an expert witness who spoke Republican jurists' language. Ken Starr—the man Republicans trusted to impeach a president—could have read from his law review article the section that said "ordering a new election. . . when the results of the prior one are suspicious comports with the duties of [the courts] both to sit as tribunals of equity, balancing competing considerations, and to serve as the principle protectors of constitutionally guaranteed rights."

Even Starr would have been on a fool's mission, however. Labarga was not budging. Expert witnesses, legal precedents, and the demands of democracy meant nothing. That was obvious when he issued a decision stating that he lacked the authority to call a new election. "Given the uniqueness of presidential elections and the undue advantage a revote or a new vote may afford one candidate over the other, it was the clear and unambiguous intention of the framers of the Constitution of the United States that presidential elections be held on a single date throughout the United States." Never mind that, in all of the elections for president that took place during the lifetimes of the framers of the Constitution, ballots were cast on multiple dates. And never mind the fact that a revote was needed precisely because the initial balloting had afforded one candidate (George W. Bush) an undue advantage over the other (Al Gore). Labarga was not about to mess with a messed-up election. Besides, with Bush winning, the election didn't look all that messed-up to Republicans.

In a scene that owed its dramatic flavor to the law-school-nightmare film *Paper Chase,* the judge demanded the seemingly impossible of lawyers seeking a revote. "I want you to find me another case in the continental United States since the year 1776 where there's been a revote in a presidential election," he boomed from the bench. "That's my homework for you attorneys."

In the matter of hours between when Labarga made his demand and when he issued his no-revote ruling, the lawyers were not prepared to leap the high bar Labarga set for them.

But thirty-two years and a thousand miles away from Labarga's West Palm Beach courtroom, a Maryland circuit court judge had quietly resolved a similarly disquieting dispute. The presidential election of 1968—a hard-fought contest that produced a popular-vote victory for Richard Nixon even narrower than the Gore popular-vote win of 2000—was particularly contentious in Maryland. Republican Richard

Labarga indicated that he was reluctant to exercise the power he had to fix the problem

Nixon's running mate was Maryland governor Spiro Agnew. Segregationist independent George Wallace won wide support in the border state. Yet Democrat Hubert Humphrey ended up securing the state's electoral votes. Despite the intense scrutiny of the Maryland vote, election officials failed to prevent a major screwup in the Chesapeake Bay village of St. Michaels. A total of 435 local voters showed up to cast their ballots; yet when the voting machine was opened, only 14 presidential votes had been registered. Two of the good citizens of St. Michael's decided that this denial of democracy must not stand, so they sued for relief in the circuit court of Talbot County. The case landed in the courtroom of the venerable Judge Harry Clark. A no-nonsense jurist, Clark reviewed the facts before him, determined that the right of voters to register their sentiments in the election had been denied by the mechanical mishap, and ordered a revote. A week after the election, the voters of St. Michaels dutifully returned to the fire station and cast ballots that actually counted.

The lawyers were not prepared to leap the high bar Labarga set for them

The St. Michaels revote was a mere footnote to the election of 1968. It did not change the identity of the winner; indeed, there were not enough votes involved to have shifted the results for Maryland. But those are the inconsequential details of democracy. The point, as Judge Clark understood and Judge Labarga chose to deny, is that elections are not the province of politicians and parties, but of the great mass of citizens for whom democracy is only as real as the ability to cast their ballots and have them counted.

For close to 200,000 Floridians, illegal ballot designs, intimidations, and misdeeds resulted in the denial of their franchise on November 7. As befits a nation that purports to instruct the world in the proper practice of democracy, remedies were available. The best of these—a revote on ballots and machines free of the flaws that disenfranchised so many—could have been implemented in Palm Beach County, or statewide, just as it was in 1968 in that fire station in St. Michael's, Maryland.

It was in the denial of that remedy, more than in any of the other dark machinations that accompanied the long fight over Florida's votes, that the great promise of American democracy was sacrificed on the altar of partisanship.

CHAPTER 5

Homage to Katarina

"I believe that George Bush won the election through the vote of the people and the way our republic is set up. All we did was follow the law in the Department of State."
—Florida secretary of state Katherine Harris

"I thought Katherine Harris's description of her role was laughable—ha, ha, ha."
—U.S. Commission on Civil Rights chair Mary Frances Berry

When George W. Bush finished whooping it up at the Florida Republican Party's Inaugural Ball, country singer Larry Gatlin stepped to the microphone. He had not come to sing. He was there to introduce the woman whose pivotal role in securing a Republican White House made her second only to the new president on the evening's list of featured speakers:

"In France it was Joan of Arc; in the Crimea it was Florence Nightingale; in the deep south there was Rosa Parks; in India there was

"In France it was Joan of Arc . . . in Florida there was Katherine Harris"

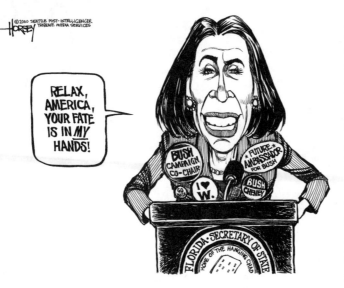

©2000 SEATTLE POST-INTELLIGENCER
TRIBUNE MEDIA SERVICES

RELAX, AMERICA, YOUR FATE IS IN *MY* HANDS!

BUSH CAMPAIGN CO-CHAIR

FUTURE AMBASSADOR FOR BUSH

I ♥ W.

BUSH CHENEY

FLORIDA · SECRETARY OF STATE

HOME OF THE HANGING CHAD

Mother Teresa," Gatlin told the whooping-it-up crowd. "And in Florida there was Katherine Harris."

The Rosa Parks reference could well be the most distasteful of the entire Florida debacle—considering the role Harris played in disenfranchising thousands of African-American voters in Florida. But Gatlin's introduction, however far it flew over the top, illustrated that, for Republicans, Harris was no bureaucratic bit player; she was the woman who plucked the presidency from the jaws of defeat and handed it to the man she had previously declared herself "thrilled and honored" to support.

"Those 36 days elevated Katherine," Florida Republican Party chairman Al Cardenas explained. "She's the darling of Republicans throughout the country." Florida Senate Republican leader Jim King added, "I've had people call and say, 'Give her a limousine and let her do anything she wants.'"

The notion that a secretary of state, the political equivalent of the school librarian, would be elevated to such vaunted status may seem bizarre. But, then, Harris was responsible for a bizarre stretch of the job description. In most American states, secretaries of state are charged with overseeing the election process. Most of them are elected, and most are titularly affiliated with one party or another. But few have ever blurred the lines of partisanship so dramatically as did Harris before, during, and after the 2000 election. No comedian commenting on the 2000 election came up with a funnier line than Harris's claim that she had erected "a firewall to make sure that everything was conducted without any partisanship during the recount." In fact, Harris never deviated from the Bush campaign playbook during the recount process—as anyone who had watched her campaign enthusiastically for George W. Bush throughout the year 2000 would have predicted. Harris's obvious preference for the Republican nominee led veteran political commentator Tom Wicker to ask: "Why didn't Secretary of State Harris, a co-chairman of the Bush campaign in Florida, recuse herself from deciding the question [of] whether recounts . . . should be certified? Was a conflict of interest ever more clear?"

The conflict was beyond debate. But neither Harris nor her team of taxpayer-funded lawyers and political advisers would entertain the notion of putting propriety ahead of partisanship.

Joe Klock, Katherine Harris's attorney, characterized his client as "someone who's been caught in the headlights of history." That was the official spin of the legions of Florida fixers with close ties to Governor Jeb Bush and Harris who went out of their way to paint the compromised secretary of state as an innocent bystander swept into the maelstrom of political intrigue. And, while no one was buying the innocent line, plenty of national observers accepted the notion of Harris as an inept pawn in a chess game being played by a savvier set of partisans. In a bizarre miscalculation, Washington reporters, pundits, and Gore campaign operatives were only too happy to run with the cliché of the ditzy debutante who had fallen into a pool of political sharks—an underestimation that Harris and the Republicans masterfully exploited.

Throughout the recount fight, Harris gave few interviews, and when she did, the secretary of state frequently steered the conversation toward discussion of her looks—knowing all too well the advan-

> "Was a conflict of interest ever more clear?"
>
> —TOM WICKER

tage of being judged a minor player in so high stakes a struggle. With the aid of a team of political strategists and public relations professionals—including Florida pros, former managers of New York mayor Rudy Giuliani's campaigns, and a top aide to John McCain's presidential quest—Harris ran one of the most sophisticated political operations of the year 2000. She used her office and taxpayer funds to promote Bush's candidacy before and after November 7, she seeded key decision-making positions with Republicans and—ingeniously—conservative Democrats aligned with Bush, she made rigid decisions where flexibility was in order, she shifted deadlines to exclude unwanted returns, she permitted recounts that favored Gore to be ignored, she misplaced vital documents at critical stages of the process, all the while deflecting attention from her actions with a combination of "official" statements from flag-bedecked podiums and *Seventeen* magazine chatter carefully calculated to accentuate an already absurdly overblown focus on her clothes, her hair, and above all, her makeup. When Democratic strategist Paul Begala compared her with Cruella DeVil, a giggling Harris announced, "I love Dalmatians." When the male talking heads of television derided her generous application of eyeliner and lipstick, Harris noted gleefully that "the guys were wearing much more makeup than I was." When she sat down for the inevitable "serious"

Harris ran one of the most sophisticated political operations of the year 2000

Co-chair of the Florida Bush-for-President campaign.

interviews, Harris repeated variations on the story of a late night visit to a grocery store or Target—depending on the interview—where she ran into a woman in a food aisle or a checkout line—depending on the interview—who asked if she was in fact "the" Katherine Harris. No matter what the lead-up, the punch line was always the same, always perfectly delivered: "Yeah, I only have on one layer of makeup. I'm incognito."

While "professional" pundits and politicos argued if maybe it was Maybelline that made Harris look the way she did, one of the savviest and most successful political climbers in Florida's recent history ruthlessly calculated and then implemented a series of deft moves that made a Bush presidency not merely possible but inevitable. One of the few political commentators who "got" Harris was *Atlanta Constitution* editorial page editor Cynthia Tucker, a veteran observer of southern politics who laughed off the "misread" of the secretary of state by Gore aides who called Harris a "hack" and a "lackey." "She is no mere flunky carrying water for higher-ups," Tucker slyly observed of Harris. "Girlfriend has a game plan with her own ambitions at the center."

She used her office and taxpayer funds to promote Bush's candidacy before and after November 7

Katherine Harris was born with a game plan. She is a daughter of her state's political aristocracy. Indeed, she is far more deeply rooted in Florida's political landscape than newcomers such as Jeb Bush. Where most of the prime players in the Florida debacle had to scramble to maps to figure out where contested counties such as Pasco and Polk were located, Harris came from a family that pretty much owned those counties—and much of the rest of central Florida.

A fourth-generation Floridian, with family ties more tangled than those of a Kennedy in Massachusetts and a personal history of daring political leaps and cutthroat tactics, Harris was a new name only to those who had never paid serious attention to the internecine twists and turns of Sunshine State politics—a group, it seems, that included the entire national media corps and just about anyone with decision-making authority on Al Gore's recount team.

Harris was neither Jeb Bush's personal or political concubine, nor was she a simple Sarasota socialite taking her orders from Austin. Truth be told:

☞ Katherine Harris is a political heiress. Her maternal grandfather, Ben Hill Griffin, Jr., a subject of John McPhee's 1967 book *Oranges*, parlayed a 10-acre orange grove into a 375,000-acre agribusiness empire valued at the time of his death in 1990 at $300 million. Griffin built his empire the old-fashioned way—by writing the laws that regulated it. He represented Polk County in the Florida legislature during the 1950s and 1960s, before the federal Voting Rights Act broke the stranglehold of rural legislators over Florida policy making. During those times, according to Florida writer E. Garrett Youngblood, "On citrus, his word was law—literally. A political writer once noted that amending a Ben Hill Griffin citrus bill 'would be like amending the book of Genesis.'" Not surprisingly, conditions for African American citrus workers did not dramatically improve during the 1950s and 1960s. Nor did their children get much help from Griffin, who worked with fellow segregationist Democrats to keep schools separate and unequal. Griffin's final foray into electoral politics was a last-stand-for-Dixie challenge to moderate "New South" Governor Reuben Askew in the 1974 Democratic primary. Soon after, Griffin family campaign contributions began powering Republican campaigns. In his last years, old Ben Hill devoted himself to writing multi-million-dollar checks to the University of Florida— the football field, though known as "the swamp," is actually named for him, as is the Ben Hill Griffin, Jr., Citrus Research and Education

Center—and to doting on the granddaughter who was born the year he first went to the legislature.

Grandpa set Katherine's father up as the chairman of the local Citrus and Commercial Bank, peopled family gatherings with governors and senators who would eventually help her enter politics, and made sure that even after his passing she would be taken care of—and guided—by him. An inheritance from her grandfather made Katherine Harris independently wealthy—she's worth an estimated $6.6 million—and her political career has been financed and aided from its start by allies of her late granddad. One of her most vocal defenders during the whole recount flap was Florida Republican National Committeeman Tom Slade—who dutifully informed reporters in his official capacity that "if Katherine's star was rising before, it has shot up like a rocket now, at least in the party." Only a few old-timers recalled that Slade had been a friend of Ben Hill Griffin, Jr., or that he had known Katherine Harris since she was a little girl riding a horse named Cracker across her grandfather's central Florida empire. While Gore campaign aide Mark Fabiani was calling Harris "a crony of the Bush brothers," savvy Floridians such as Marc Dunbar were pointing out—to little notice from the national press—that "she tapped into a very lucrative network through her grandfather long before [Jeb] Bush was ever elected."

☞ Katherine Harris is one of the most brazenly ambitious and bloodthirsty political players in Florida. She's "a masterful hardball politician," according to Ron Sachs, an aide to former Florida governor Lawton Chiles. National pundits referred to her having been "actively" involved in politics for only six years at the time of the recount, missing the supreme irony that George W. Bush had entered politics the same year Harris did. By most measures, however, Harris

"Harris is a masterful hardball politician"

—FLORIDA POLITICO RON SACHS

was far better prepared than George W. for the big time. After earning a degree in history from Georgia's toney Agnes Smith College, Harris studied art and Spanish at the University of Madrid, read philosophy and religion at universities in Geneva, and collected a masters in public administration degree with an emphasis in international trade from Harvard. She worked for a number of years as a marketing executive for IBM in Tampa, Dallas, and finally New York before taking a post as vice president of a commercial real estate company on Florida's booming Gulf Coast. A few years later, with advice from Tom Slade and others, she challenged the Democratic state senator from Sarasota. After raising an unprecedented $500,000 for her race, the first-time candidate beat the veteran pol handily with a blistering negative advertising campaign.

Four years later, she took on incumbent Republican secretary of state Sandra Mortham, in the party's 1998 primary. Jeb Bush and most of the state's Republican establishment backed Mortham, but Harris hired J. M. "Mac the Knife" Stipanovich, a legendary Florida Republican operative, who compares campaigns to Vietnam firefights, to help her craft a go-for-the-jugular strategy. Harris then sat on her campaign money until the final days of the campaign, when she unleashed a savage $800,000 television attack-ad campaign in which she accused the incumbent of campaign finance violations involving a corporation that had, in fact, given far larger sums to Harris. The *St. Petersburg Times* called Harris's attack campaign "one of the most cynical tactics of this election year." But it worked with GOP primary voters, who handed Harris an easy win.

After declaring that she was prepared for a calm, issue-oriented fall contest against her Democratic foe, Miami children's advocate Karen Gievers, Harris then ran television ads attacking Gievers as a "liberal lobbyist" who "leads an extremist group with an ultra-feminist agenda." What exactly was Gievers' radical record? She had worked with groups seeking to elect more women to public office and was an unpaid lobbyist for foster mothers and for Operation SafeDrive—a program she started after a teenage driver struck and killed her husband while he was riding a bike.

Despite criticism from the state's daily newspapers for her twisting of the truth, Harris won the race by a 55 to 45 margin. She celebrated her victory by declaring that, while the secretary of state's job was to be eliminated in 2003, she would not use her new post as a "stepping stone" to higher office. In March 1999, two months after she was sworn in as secretary of state, Harris announced that she was thinking of running for Florida's open U.S. Senate seat. She opted instead to take a high-profile role in the Bush family's campaign to reclaim the White House, feeding speculation that she would seek a Florida U.S. House seat in 2002, challenge U.S. senator Bob Graham in 2004, or join the Bush administration. As Tom Slade, Grandpa Ben Hill Griffin's pal, told national reporters, "She is talented, articulate, very attractive, and has enormous personal wealth. She will have a great many opportunities."

☞ Katherine Harris knows how to get around the rules and regulations of campaigns and elections. Since she entered politics, Harris has been trailed by constant scandal. Her 1994 state senate campaign involved campaign finance misdeeds so serious that the Sarasota *Herald-Tribune* referred to the Harris candidacy as "a snapshot of what

Harris has been trailed by constant scandal

Harris's
campaign
finance law
violations
were
investigated
by the Florida
Department
of Law
Enforcement

can happen when a candidate heavily courts money and gets it."
Officials with Riscorp Inc., a workers compensation insurer, came up
with what they thought was an ingenious plan to gain legislative favor
for their company: They would subvert campaign finance laws by giving bonuses to employees who would then donate the money to
favored candidates in the company's name. The whole endeavor was a
gross violation of Florida campaign finance laws, and it was eventually
exposed in a scandal that resulted in the convictions of the company's
founder and other top employees. Harris was a prime recipient of
Riscorp money, collecting $20,600 in contributions. In addition,
Riscorp officials hired an independent consultant to aide Harris's campaign and paid the tab for a Harris fund-raising event that mysteriously
went unreported on campaign finance filings. Documents obtained
from Riscorp included a memo that read, "Katherine's office called
and asked if we could give them different addresses to list for each of
the checks." Harris's campaign manager was identified as an unindicted
co-conspirator in the scandal. Harris's involvement was investigated by
the Florida Department of Law Enforcement. Particularly damning
for Harris was the revelation that, once she got to the Senate, she
immediately filed bills and amendments sought by the company. Harris
claimed the legislative proposals were "good public policy." When the
heat was on, however, she told reporters in a quivering voice, "I and so
many other public officials fell victim to fraudulent activities of someone else. There's no way I knew or any of us could have known what
was going on behind the scenes." In the same year she made that statement, Harris attacked Secretary of State Sandra Mortham's ties to
Riscorp, even though links between Mortham and the discredited corporation were far less significant than her own.

That wasn't Harris's only scandal. As a state senator, she failed to
file required financial-disclosure forms for so long that she was threat-

ened with civil penalties. Of 160 Florida legislators, all but two got their forms in before Harris.

The Harris record was such that, when she sought the secretary of state's post, Common Cause of Florida vice president Lloyd Brumfield wondered how she could credibly enforce campaign finance and ethics laws overseen by the office. "In essence [as secretary of state], she would be the cop. How can you come down on somebody else for violating something when you have a reputation for violating the law yourself?" When Harvard law professor Alan Dershowitz labeled Harris "a crook," he was roundly criticized for treating the secretary of state unfairly. In fact, Dershowitz's only mistake was to arrive in Florida with more knowledge of Harris's past than most newcomers.

☞ Except in an instance when the whole world was watching—as with the 2000 recount— Katherine Harris could not be bothered with the mundane duties of overseeing elections. The *St. Petersburg Times* editorial board opined during her 1998 campaign that, while the candidate had some interesting ideas regarding arts programs, "Harris seems less interested in the office's central role in the state's election process." As soon as Harris took office, electoral responsibilities—with the exception of a state initiative costing almost $4 million to purge voter rolls of former felons and other "undesirables"—took a backseat as the new secretary of state took to the road. Declaring her intention to "transform the Department of State into Florida's State Department," Harris embarked on 10 overseas treks in 20 months. In her first year and half in office—precisely the time when she should have been meticulously overseeing preparations for the 2000 elections—Harris flew off to Mexico, Panama, Brazil, Venezuela, Canada, Argentina, Barbados, and Australia. Her travel expenses for her first 22 months in office came to $106,808, three times the expenditure for Florida gover-

She failed to file required financial-disclosure forms for so long that she was threatened with civil penalties

nor Jeb Bush. The *St. Petersburg Times* said, "She has quickly become a Florida version of Madeleine Albright, the globe-trotting U.S. secretary of state." Just weeks before the election, Harris could not be found in Jacksonville or Miami. Why? She was in Sydney, Australia, debuting the state's $700,000 "Florida World Pavilion" at the 2000 Summer Olympics. Was Harris promoting the Sunshine State or herself? As Canada Press noted, "She has done nothing to squelch speculation that she's interested in an ambassador's job from a George W. Bush White House." Actually, Harris let slip during the 2000 campaign that she was "passionately interested" in a foreign affairs gig—particularly one involving international trade negotiations, her area of focus at Harvard. To that end, she launched a bizarre campaign out of the secretary of state's office to have Miami named the permanent headquarters for the Free Trade Area of the Americas. When she wasn't in Toronto or Buenos Aires, Harris was booked into the $332-a-night Willard-Intercontinental Hotel in Washington for meetings with foreign ambassadors and members of Congress to discuss trade policy—she traveled to the Capitol more than a dozen times during 1999 and 2000—or at New York's $485-a-night Barbizon for sessions of the Council on Foreign Relations.

All this official travel left little time for mundane chores, such as sessions with local and state elections officials. In a state with some of the most disjointed and—as the 2000 election illustrated—dysfunctional electoral processes, Harris couldn't really be bothered with the intricacies of election reform. "Even top Republicans say Harris has shown little interest in the election side of her job," reported *Washington Post* reporters Dana Milbank and Jo Becker during the recount battle. And a *Time* magazine review of her record revealed that "both GOP and Democratic state legislators say that Harris, as secretary of state, has shown little interest in electoral-reform bills—despite taking office

"Even top Republicans say Harris has shown little interest in the election side of her job"

—THE WASHINGTON POST

after one of the state's worst cases of election fraud, one that saw a Miami mayoral race overturned in court."

County election supervisors, the people who could have saved Florida from the fall 2000 embarrassment, grouse that Harris rarely attends their meetings. That complaint surfaced even more loudly when the secretary of state's office began to point fingers of blame at local elections officials during the recount process. While veteran poll watchers had complained for years about flaws in the state's systems for casting and counting ballots, Harris called the whole mess "an extraordinary lesson in civics." Despite testimony from Leon County supervisor of elections Ion Sancho that the state's refusal to provide $100,000 in requested voter-education funding had made the jobs of local elections officials tougher, Harris would tell the U.S. Civil Rights Commission that, as the state's chief elections official, she was unaware of serious concerns about voter education or requests from elections supervisors for extra assistance in anticipation of high turnouts on November 7. The commission chair called her testimony "laughable," and rightly so. Harris was deeply involved with the Bush campaign in the run-up to the election; thus, she could not have been unaware of Republican concerns regarding high turnout predictions for predominantly African American and Jewish precincts. Yet, the sole election-related statement from Harris's office in the week before the vote did not call for stepped-up efforts to manage higher than usual levels of participation. Rather, her office issued a strange four-paragraph missive assuring voters that rumors circulating on the Internet about having Republicans vote on Wednesday, November 8, the day after the election, were "false and a poor attempt at humor."

Odd as it might have been, the statement was, for Harris, a rarity— an official comment regarding a Florida election issued by her office

She could not have been unaware of Republican concerns regarding high turnout predictions

and under her name before the November 7 vote. Of the press statements released by Harris's office so far during her tenure, the overwhelming majority have referenced global concerns—including an extended commentary from the Floridian on mudslides in Venezuela.

What luck then for Harris that the Bush team, when things got hot in Florida, dispatched a foreign-affairs soul mate. Former secretary of state James Baker was a prime architect of U.S. foreign policy and international trade strategies under George Bush the Elder and, by extension, the Clinton and Bush the Younger administrations. Indeed, Baker's protégé, Robert Zoellick, would soon become the new Bush administration's U.S. trade representative. Baker was understanding and helpful to Harris when—even as she was managing the election and its recount for the Bush family—the secretary of state was simultaneously attempting to organize the World Economic Forum's first hemisphere-wide Financial Conference for the Americas in Tallahassee. It couldn't have hurt Harris's ego when William Perry, a former Reagan administration official and Baker compatriot who was advising the Bush transition team on Latin American policy, showed up to meet with the Floridian regarding her favorite trade issues. And what a boost, during the very week when Harris was setting the deadline for certifying the state's electors, to have Perry tell Florida reporters that "someone in [Harris's] position could have influence on our Latin American policy. And I hope to hell she does." No wonder that, even as pundits dismissed Harris's prospects as a potential Bush administration ambassador or trade representative, she continued to delight in the speculation. "Certainly," she told Diane Sawyer, who asked about an ambassadorship, "that is a dream of everyone."

☞ In an epic abuse of her authority, Katherine Harris regularly used her position to promote voter turnout on behalf of George W.

Harris regularly used her position to promote voter turnout on behalf of George W. Bush

Bush. Harris was never the Jeb Bush acolyte that Gore campaigners and television talking heads made her out to be, but she was a very loyal Republican. She served proudly with Jeb as an at-large member of the Florida GOP's state executive board, assiduously making the rounds of county party dinners and even lending "official" credibility to the "Republican Party of Florida Switch Roadshow." The latter initiative saw Harris traveling the state in 1999 with a huge and hokey Republican party registration card that she and Republican National Committee chair Jim Nicholson presented to Democrats who had shifted their affiliation. Harris's real energy, however, would soon be directed into the more glamorous field of presidential politicking.

An early and very enthusiastic backer of the Bush-for-President campaign, Harris in the fall of 1999 posted an endorsement of the Texas governor on his presidential campaign web site and accepted the title of Florida Bush-for-President campaign co-chair. That an official charged with overseeing elections in a highly competitive state would take the lead in the campaign of a particular contender was appalling to former Texas secretary of state Ron Kirk: "I think Ms. Harris exercised . . . horrible judgment in deciding to take an active role in the Bush campaign."

"Active" is precisely the right word. In January 2000, she and Jeb Bush flew with 138 other Floridians to New Hampshire, where, in a failed effort to derail Arizonan John McCain's successful primary challenge to Bush, they donned "Freezin' for a Reason" badges and trooped door to door in the cold to deliver Florida strawberries and oranges to startled New Hampshireites.

By the time Republicans gathered in Philadelphia to nominate a presidential candidate, Harris was a high-profile Bush delegate, camped out at the swank Loew's Hotel. At the convention Harris hooked up with retired general Norman Schwarzkopf, who lives in the Tampa area; soon, she had enlisted the general to appear at Bush

"I think Ms. Harris exercised . . . horrible judgment in deciding to take an active role in the Bush campaign"

—FORMER TEXAS SECRETARY OF STATE RON KIRK

rallies around Florida, a state with a huge population of military retirees, and to record get-out-the-vote phone messages for Republicans. Harris then initiated a public-private political partnership that would have been unimaginable in most states. At the same time that Schwarzkopf was openly endorsing Bush, the Florida secretary of state's office allocated $30,000 from its budget to produce a 30-second public service announcement in which the general made a "nonpartisan" go-vote appeal. (Bush's name wasn't mentioned in the taxpayer-funded commercials, but given the general's association with the Bush campaign, columnist Joe Conason rightly argued that a Schwarzkopf get-out-the-vote call "didn't have to say for whom.") Common Cause and other groups condemned the last-minute diversion of scarce election funds for so obviously partisan a purpose, especially at a time when county elections officials were worrying aloud about whether they could manage the surge in turnout on Election Day. Ordering the ads aired was Harris's final preelection contribution to George W. Bush's campaign.

Postelection, she would significantly up the ante.

"The process of counting and recounting the votes cast on Election Day must end."

—Florida secretary of state Katherine Harris setting the deadline for certifying George W. Bush's "win" in Florida

"Somehow, the media has subscribed to the notion that Gore should concede and Bush is the winner. Gore should not concede until the votes are counted."

—Former Ohio secretary of state Sherrod Brown

The Bush-for-President campaign had two primary purposes in the weeks following the too-close-to-call finish in Florida: to maintain the illusion that Bush had won the November 7 election and to foster the fantasy that Al Gore was not playing by the rules when he asked Florida officials to count every vote. No matter what the latest development in the campaign, the Bush camp reverted to message, with the candidate, his aides, his lawyers, former secretary of state James Baker, and congressional and gubernatorial "surrogates" constantly claiming that all ballots in Florida had been counted, that hand recounts were more fallible than machine counts, and that politics—as opposed to a desire to identify the true winner of a presidential election—was preventing the completion of the process. No matter how loudly Gore called for an honest count, the Bush camp shouted more loudly that the Democrat was somehow corrupting the process. The vice president argued for a complete count, saying, "I would not want to win the presidency by a few votes cast in error or misinterpreted or not counted. And I don't think Governor Bush wants that either. So, having enough patience to spend the days necessary to hear exactly what the American people have said is really the most important thing, because that is what honors our Constitution and redeems the promise of our democracy." Bush spokeswoman Karen Hughes responded, "The vice president basically said we should ignore the law so he can overturn the results of the election."

Stationed in Florida as pointman and chief enforcer for the Bush recount fight, James Baker could repeat the mantra even while reviewing complex documents, and he never failed to suggest—mustering all of the authority of a former Bush and Reagan administration cabinet secretary— that it was his measured conclusion that the stability of the

No matter what the latest development in the campaign, the Bush camp reverted to message

Ready for her close-up. Harris once again explaining her principled, independent, entirely nonpartisan decision to reject hand recounts of ballots.

republic, or at least the Nasdaq index, would be endangered unless all vote counting immediately ceased, enabling Harris to certify George W. Bush as the nation's president-elect. "It is time to bring this to a close," was Baker's standard retort to any and all questions—even, locals joked, to inquiries regarding the weather. "Baker keeps acting as though there's some phantom populace impatiently demanding a swift resolution," wrote columnist Maureen Dowd. "That's simply not true," she added, echoing polling data that showed Americans were more interested in an honest count than a quick conclusion to the contest.

The Bush campaign's campaign for "closure" would have been written off as a comic exercise in partisan scaremongering were it not for the official sanction it received from Harris. Florida's Republican secretary of state appeared regularly before television cameras during the 36 days of wrangling over the count—usually in front of red-white-and-blue bunting—to assert that the rules required a quick end to the count, even if accuracy had to be sacrificed. Harris claimed the law tied her hands, and that partisanship had nothing to do with her pronouncements. "I want to reassure the public my decisions in this process have been made carefully, consistently, independently, and I believe correctly," she declared.

Careful and consistent, Harris was. But "independent" and "correct"? Forget about it. Democratic vice presidential nominee Joe Lieberman said Harris appeared to be determined to "decide the election herself." Florida Democratic Party chair Bob Poe was more blunt, saying, "It becomes clearer and clearer with every action she takes, every statement she makes, that [Harris] is still the co-chairman of the Bush campaign of Florida and not our secretary of state." And it wasn't just partisans who were complaining. The *St. Petersburg Times*, perhaps the state's most highly regarded newspaper, accused Harris of "indifference to the credibility of her office and the integrity of Florida's election process." University of Wisconsin political science professor Don Kettl, one of the nation's leading specialists on state government said that "[Watching Harris's handling of the crisis] reminds us how deeply wired politics is in any political decision and how hard it is to separate political loyalties from even technical decisions."

During the entire 36-day struggle, the Florida secretary of state consistently echoed the Bush–Baker "we won—case closed" mantra in her public statements or her interpretation of the rules for recounts. Veteran Florida political observer Ron Sachs marveled at her focus and precision under "extraordinary pressure," noting that "she's made sure that every move she makes says, 'I'll be damned if I'm the one who's going to get blamed for costing George W. Bush the election.'"

There was an assumption on the part of her critics that Harris was under constant direction from the Bush campaign. Critic Poe charged, "It's my guess that she gets a substantial portion of her marching orders right out of Austin." But it was less a matter of the Bush camp pulling Harris's strings than of Harris collaborating with the bad boys from Texas. The extent of this collaboration was evident from the start. A call was placed from Harris's cell phone to the Texas governor's mansion at 11:50 P.M. on election night, when Harris was attending a tense Bush "victory" rally in Tallahassee, and Jeb and George Bush were hunkered down in Austin. Less than six hours later, Harris acknowledges that she was stirred from sleep at home by a call from

Lieberman said Harris appeared to be determined to "decide the election herself"

> **"THOSE WHO CAST THE VOTES DECIDE NOTHING.**
> **THOSE WHO COUNT THE VOTES**
> **DECIDE EVERYTHING."**
>
> **—JOSEPH STALIN**

Jeb Bush telling her to hightail it over to the secretary of state's office because there was going to be a recount. But, while there should be no doubt that the collusion between the secretary of state and top Republican operatives was frequent and critical to the success of the campaign's success, Harris did not have to be told the essential thrust of the strategy; whenever a question of policy arose, Harris knew she simply had to make the call most beneficial to Bush.

☞ Harris began by putting the "right" people in the right places. Tallahassee is a Democratic town, which Al Gore won overwhelmingly. Veteran state employees in the secretary of state's office tended toward the "D" side of the political ledger. "I bet probably half of them voted for Gore," Harris's personal lawyer, Joseph Klock, said of the lawyers working in the office. But Harris assured that top decision-making slots were filled with Republicans, or Democrats who placed loyalty to the Bush clan ahead of party ties. When Harris took over as secretary of state in 1999, she did not select a career staffer from inside the department to head the Division of Elections. Rather she chose L. Clayton Roberts, a registered Republican from the staff of the state legislature, where she had served in the Republican majority. In the middle of the recount fight, the *Miami Herald* reported that Roberts was taking calls—and marching orders?—from Frank Jimenez, the acting general counsel for Jeb Bush whom veteran Tallahassee lobbyist

Ron Brook refers to as the Republican governor's "emissary." In addition to overseeing the day-to-day work of purging voter rolls and approving the use of butterfly ballots, Roberts sat with Harris on the Florida Elections Canvassing Commission, which would certify George W. Bush as the winner of the state's 25 electoral votes.

The third member of the canvassing commission, one Jeb Bush, was obliged to recuse himself, as it was thought unseemly for Brother No. 1 to select Brother No. 2 to serve as president. In replacing Jeb Bush, Harris opted for what looked like bipartisanship, naming Florida secretary of agriculture Bob Crawford, a Democrat, to the commission. Crawford, a good old boy of the first order, had worked his way up the Florida political ladder over the past quarter century, serving as president of the state Senate before winning the politically powerful agriculture gig.

Though he ran for election as a Democrat, Crawford developed a penchant for endorsing Republicans—especially if it looked like they were going to win. In 1998, he had backed Jeb Bush over Democrat Buddy MacKay for governor. In 2000, he jumped on board the George W. Bush bandwagon, even appearing at rallies around the state with the Republican presidential candidate. Thus, while national media reports dutifully recorded Crawford's party affiliation as "Democrat," Harris knew him to be a solid vote for her shut-down-the-count-before-it-produces-a-Gore-victory schemes. Crawford was not concerned about offending fellow Democrats in a way that might hurt him at the ballot box; after delivering the presidency to Bush, he left his elective post to take a lucrative agribusiness industry position.

Crawford wasn't the only titular Democrat creating the false impression of bipartisanship on the secretary of state's team. Though her office had plenty of lawyers on staff, Harris hired the Miami law firm of Steel, Hector and Davis—which counted among its former partners then–attorney general Janet Reno—to advise and represent her

Harris began by putting the "right" people in the right places

personally during the recount process. Joe Klock, who headed the 13-member team working with Harris, describes himself as a "passionate Democrat." That, he told reporters, ought to serve as evidence of Harris's evenhanded approach. "The Democrats would have her as some sort of pawn for the Bush campaign," Klock argued. "But if that were the case, then she would have reached out to a Republican firm. The fact is, she reached out to us." The twist, of course, is that Klock's Democratic passions wax and wane with the political winds. He attends the same Miami church as Jeb Bush, whom he supported for governor in 1998. On election night, "passionate Democrat" Klock e-mailed a message of congratulations to Jeb. Later, for a giggle, Klock sent a retraction —à la Gore's withdrawal of his concession. The Klock firm's legal work for his "friend" Katherine Harris paid a cool $682,266—the single highest expenditure of the entire recount.

The most critical staffing decision made by the secretary of state at the onset of the recount process involved herself. When calls came from academics and newspapers for Harris to recuse herself from the process because of her record as a Bush partisan, the secretary dismissed the suggestions as mere partisanship on the part of Democrats. She was the elected secretary of state, she said, and it was her duty to "effectuate the public's right to clarity and finality." In this, she had the support of the only man who could have told her to step aside. Asked if it was appropriate for a Bush campaign co-chair to oversee the recount that would decide the presidency, Governor Jeb Bush concluded, "I think it's more than appropriate for a secretary of state, who is responsible for the election law in our state."

☞ Harris perfected her spin. The secretary of state and her aides told reporters that they had erected a "fire wall" between her office and the Republican party and the Bush campaign. But Republican

Republican political strategists were meeting regularly with Harris to hone her public image

political strategists were meeting regularly with Harris to hone her approach to the dispute. Equally disingenuous was the fantasy, fostered by Harris, that she was so immune to the pull of PR that her office operated without a press secretary through most of 2000. While technically true, Harris—a former Fortune

500 marketing executive—did not exactly toss herself unprotected into the postelection media frenzy. She started by calling in longtime advisers, such as "Mac the Knife" Stipanovich and Grandpa Ben Hill Griffin's pal Tom Slade. And when the stakes grew, she hired the big guns. Adam Goodman, owner of the Victory Group, a top Republican campaign consulting firm, arrived shortly after November 7 to give what Harris chief of staff Ben McKay described as "dos and don'ts." "It was not related to decision making or substance," McKay claimed, "but rather, how to do it." The "how-to" talks included a consultation by the GOP strategist with the "above partisanship" secretary of state on the evening before she announced she would stick to her controversial deadline for certifying election results from counties around the state.

The next day found Harris in the midst of a political firestorm. Court challenges were launched. Circumspect Senator Joe Lieberman accused the secretary of state of election tipping. Comedian Jay Leno told his national television audience it was so cold in Florida that Katherine

Two days after the Supreme Court's December 12th ruling, state officials reflect on being entrusted with the solemn duty of assuring a fair count of Florida's presidential election ballots.

Harris "wore a third layer of makeup." And newspapers started digging up folks who knew Harris during her unfortunate spin as a chicken-dance instructor. At this point, the secretary called in an out-of-state political gunslinger named Dan Schnur. Once the press secretary for California governor Pete Wilson, Schnur was fresh from having served as California spokesman for John McCain's Republican presidential bid. One of the savviest political strategists in the business, Schnur understood Harris instantly. She was, he told reporter Jake Tapper, "the exact opposite of caricature"—a woman who "clearly knew her job."

While Goodman and Schnur gave behind-the-scenes and generally unreported advice to Harris, other top Republicans rushed to her defense. "I am offended by the partisan attacks on her integrity," chirped Ohio governor Bob Taft. Kansas governor Bill Graves called a press conference in Tampa to declare himself "terribly troubled by these character assassinations" of Harris. Fresh from a telephone briefing with top Bush strategists, where they had been told that the spin of the day was "Harris is being attacked by the Gore campaign in order to undermine public confidence in the process," both Graves and Taft publicly pronounced Harris "objective."

☞ Harris declared herself a rules girl. You won't find Katherine Harris's name on the Standing Committee on Elections and Voter Participation of the National Association of Secretaries of State.

Before the 2000 election she was notoriously uninterested in electoral rules and regulations to such an extent that, after the 2000 election, it was revealed that she was registered to vote in two different Florida counties. But when it fell to her personally to decide how Florida's election rules would affect George W. Bush's presidential prospects, Harris became a stickler for procedure. Funny how all the rules ended up favoring Bush. Testifying later before the U.S. Civil Rights Commission, Harris and her aides said they were merely following the law as laid down by the legislature. Her official remarks during the recount fight were thick with lines like "the criteria is clearly set forth in Florida case law" and "the reasons given in [the requests of counties for more time to conduct recounts] are insufficient to warrant waiver of the unambiguous deadline imposed by the Florida legislature." Yet even Harris had to know these statements were false. Florida laws and court precedents give the secretary of state tremendous leeway. The language Harris herself used to deny three counties permission to conduct manual recounts on November 16 indicates the latitude she knew she had. She even referred to her decision "to exercise my discretion."

Harris found "rules" where no one had seen them before—"rules" that defied logic. At one point, she penned an opinion that questioned whether ballots could even be recounted in the absence of evidence of a computer malfunction, overlooking the fact that the state's recount provisions preceded the introduction of computerized vote tabulation. On November 14, she told Warren Christopher, a Gore lieutenant, that, yes, Florida law did allow the secretary of state to waive the certification deadline under some circumstances. "But," she added, "a close election, regardless of the identity of the candidates, is not such a circumstance." While Harris prattled on about the necessity of "finality," Christopher, himself a former U.S. secretary of state, said, "Her plan, I'm afraid, has the look of an effort to produce a particular result in

"Her plan, I'm afraid, has the look of an effort to produce a particular result in the election"

—WARREN CHRISTOPHER

Ralph Nader turned out in a tuxedo.

Katherine Harris donned a designer dress.

It was spring 2001. George W. Bush was in his White House. Al Gore was teaching journalism in New York. And members of the White House Correspondents Association—the most prestigious political journalists in America—were gathered in the Washington Hilton ballroom for their annual dinner. The whole point of the affair is journalistic one-upmanship, and in this age of notoriety-knows-best, the ultimate coup at a correspondents' dinner is to seat the most controversial celebrities at your table.

Business Week won hands down, seating Nader and Harris next to one another. Nader, the consumer activist who dared run to the left of Gore on the Green Party ticket in 2000, is the man Democrats love to hate for running a progressive populist campaign that took enough votes from Al Gore to put Florida in reach of George W. Bush's otherwise failed candidacy. Harris is the Florida secretary of state Democrats love to hate for rigging the recount just enough to finish the job.

Now, finally, *Business Week* had organized the first real debate of the 2000 campaign: a face-off involving the Green and the Gator over who really gored Gore. And, unlike the three faux debates between Gore and Bush in the previous fall, this one got straight to the heart of the matter.

"More people blame me," Nader told the table, reportedly gesturing toward himself.

"No way," Harris shot back. "More people blame me!" the impartial election overseer gleefully exclaimed.

Give this one to Harris. Even if Nader put Bush in the zone, it was the secretary of state who moved the target enough so that Bush could hit it. Besides, in a democracy, everyone's got a right to run. Only election officials have the ability to decide who wins.

the election [rather] than to ensure that the voice of all the citizens of the state would be heard. It also looks like a move in the direction of partisan politics and away from the nonpartisan administration of the election laws."

The amazing thing was the amount of time it took for Christopher to catch on. Like other Democrats, he was exceptionally slow when it came to recognizing the full extent of Harris's partisan manipulations.

From the beginning of the recount process, Harris was certifying counts, constraining recounts, and suing to defend her "duty" to thwart the will of the people on a daily basis. She showed a marked penchant for misreading the word "may" as "shall" in state statutes. Again and again, the courts told her that the deadlines she imposed and the restraints she placed on local election officials were unreasonable. But Harris refused to change course simply because the law was not on her side. Harris tried to set a 5:00 P.M. deadline on the Tuesday following the election for county counts to be recorded—precluding manual recounts Gore had sought—only to have Leon County Circuit Court Judge Terry Lewis rule that the secretary of state could not arbitrarily refuse returns that arrived later than that date. The next day, Harris announced that state law did not permit her to accept amended returns and that she would certify the results of the election on November 18. The Florida Supreme Court prohibited her from imposing the deadline, and the Eleventh Circuit U.S. Court of Appeals permitted manual recounts in Broward and Palm Beach Counties to continue. Harris set a new deadline of November 26 and certified a Bush win, only to have the Florida Supreme Court reject her reading of the law and order a statewide manual recount. The revolving-door nature of the court orders and Harris's efforts to circumvent them got so absurd that, in one filing, veteran attorney Dexter Douglass, appearing for the second time in two days in the same Leon County Circuit

Courtroom, argued, "We think Katherine Harris's failure to take the direction of the court should be corrected by the court."

The Florida Supreme Court gave Harris until 9:00 A.M. Monday, November 27, to accept ballots from counties that were racing to complete difficult reexaminations of thousands of contested ballots, unless Harris's office was open on Sunday. Harris saw her opportunity to cut short the recount time by some 16 hours. Guess what? Harris announced she would make the unprecedented move of opening her office on the Sunday of the Thanksgiving holiday weekend, imposing an impossible deadline of 5:00 P.M. that day on Palm Beach County, where officials had been working through the holiday to finish the recount. As the *Palm Beach Post* newspaper noted, the secretary of state "had no taste for recounting ballots in Florida's Gore territories." When the Harris-imposed deadline arrived, the secretary of state denied a request from Palm Beach officials for a two-hour extension. (She would not even permit them the flexibility the Internal Revenue Service does when April 15 falls on a Sunday and tax filers are allowed to get their returns in on Monday without penalty.) Frustrated Palm Beach officials then attempted to submit figures from the vast majority of the county's precincts where votes had been reviewed. They beat the 5:00 P.M. deadline, but not the swift hand of Harris. She promptly rejected the figures as incomplete, denying from the official count hundreds of additional votes for Gore. Harris then certified a Bush win and, with a hand from First-Brother-to-Be Jeb, dispatched the results to the National Archives in Washington.

Harris reportedly adored the National Archives gambit, even though she had to have known she would face sanctions by the Florida Supreme Court. U.S. representative Peter Deutsch, a Florida Democrat who represents many of the as-yet uncounted voters, saw method in Harris's madness. In the middle of the mess, he said, "I honestly think

They beat the 5:00 p.m. deadline, but not the swift hand of Harris

what's going on is a strategic decision by the Bush campaign to hurt the litigation efforts" by twisting each and every court ruling to the advantage of the Republican.

☞ Harris ignored precedent, pulled strings, and colluded with the Bush campaign. While the full extent of that collusion was obscured by the destruction of data on computers in the secretary of state's office, Harris could not cover her trail of wrongdoing completely. Consider her handling of what should have been a routine request for manual recounts of contested ballots. Manual recounts had been used since the founding of Florida, not to mention in every other state in the union. Yet, when pressure for a manual recount of 2000 presidential ballots in Florida began to mount, Harris rushed to announce that the act of reviewing ballots by hand "does not produce a fair and accurate count."

When Harris feared recount results from Palm Beach County might tip the statewide tally to Gore prior to certification, she simply permitted officials in Republican-dominated Nassau County to withdraw a new count that benefited Gore. This move widened the margin for Bush at a critical stage.

Harris also appears to have encouraged an unprecedented level of collusion between the secretary of state's office and the Bush campaign. In mid-November, when Democrats went to court to challenge Harris's rulings disallowing recounts in several counties, the secretary of state's office immediately released a pair of detailed opinions supporting Harris's moves—and the Bush campaign then used those opinions as the basis for its challenge to the Democratic legal action. Democrats charged that the speed with which the secretary of state's office provided materials used by the Bush campaign, and vice versa, was evidence of massive collusion.

Manual recounts had been used since the founding of Florida

Appearing before the nation's civil rights panel, Harris offers what one commissioner called "a merry-go-round of denial."

So frustrated did Democratic lawyers grow that one of them, Frank Gummey, resorted to sarcasm, informing a Florida court that "through a stroke of luck, the Department of State has issued an opinion on this very subject today."

At every turn, Harris delivered for George W. Bush. With fellow Republicans, she proudly recounted her many official contributions to the Bush campaign. To investigators of electoral wrongdoing, however, she told a different story.

While she would gladly claim credit for Bush's win at Washington inauguration parties on January 20, testifying before the U.S. Civil Rights Commission's Tallahassee hearing in early January, Harris pulled up short. She bounced blame onto her aides and engaged in what commission member Victoria Wilson called "a merry-go-round of denial." Commission member Christopher Edley, Jr., said after Harris testified: "What is missing from these statements is [the line] 'We blew it.'"

But Florida's secretary of state didn't think she had blown anything. After all, her candidate had been sworn in as president of the United States. As far as Katherine Harris was concerned, she had done her job. Perfectly.

CHAPTER 6

The DeLay Delay

"I'm the ditch digger who makes it all happen."

—Tom DeLay on his role
in the Republican Party hierarchy

No American who is not currently occupying a seat on the U.S. Supreme Court or a statewide elective position in Florida can claim to have played a greater role in securing the presidency for George W. Bush than the bug-killing king of Fort Bend, Texas.

What with all of his responsibilities as House Republican whip, Tom DeLay doesn't get much chance to stir the old chemicals these days. But in late November 2000, the former professional exterminator spotted a passel of pests in the form of the Miami-Dade County Canvassing Board. These vermin were threatening to eat their way through the fabric of lies that claimed DeLay's Texas homeboy, W., had been elected president on November 7.

The pests had to be eliminated. DeLay had the most powerful extermination tools at his disposal—Bush campaign connections, a network of Capitol Hill aides and lobbyists, a heaping load of corporate cash,

"Mr. Gore, we will not surrender —not today, not tomorrow, not ever"

and the music of Wayne Newton to squash the recount in Miami-Dade. And, like any good exterminator, he took the necessary steps to assure the unpleasant smell that accompanied his efforts did not linger long afterward.

On the Wednesday before Thanksgiving 2000, when the eyes of the nation were fixed on the Stephen P. Clark Government Center in downtown Miami, where the local canvassing board was reviewing 10,750 uncounted ballots, a riot orchestrated by DeLay's lieutenants and carried out by his minions stopped the count. In so doing, the DeLay devotees assured that Bush Florida campaign co-chair Katherine Harris would, in her capacity as secretary of state, be able to certify a 537-vote "win" for the Republican when the recount deadline arrived. It was that certification that allowed Florida governor Jeb Bush to sign a Certificate of Ascertainment designating 25 Florida electors pledged to his brother. The paperwork was immediately transmitted to the National Archives, where it would eventually be cited by the U.S. Supreme Court in its decision to hand the presidency to George W. Bush.

Only after the certification process had been completed—effectively sealing Al Gore's fate—were the identities of the "rioters" revealed. And only with that revelation did the House whip's role in fostering the faux riot—and the ensuing Bush presidency—become obvious to even the most casual observer.

That most Americans know little of DeLay and even less of his decisive role in fixing the 2000 election result does not come as a surprise. No significant player in contemporary American politics has worked harder to avoid media celebrity than the leader of the Republican party's Taliban wing. The former terror of Houston-area termites is identified by *Fortune* magazine—no casual observer of hierarchies—as "the most powerful man in Congress," yet he rarely con-

A riot, orchestrated by DeLay's lieutenants and carried out by his minions, stopped the count

sents to extended on-the-record interviews. And he regularly asks that television cameras and tape recorders be shut off when he enters a room. As veteran Texas journalist Cragg Hines explains, DeLay avoids the cameras "so Democrats can't slap his raving into broadcast commercials." Even if DeLay—the man Republicans quietly refer to as their party's "crazy aunt in the basement"—were to slip up in public, the theory goes, the congressman's self-enforced obscurity would make it hard for Democrats to exploit the blunder. DeLay aides brag about polls showing that fewer than one in five Americans can even name their boss, let alone associate him with a political party.

DeLay was a prime player in the Republican takeover of the House in 1994 and the driving force behind much of the Republican "Contract with America"—particularly sections designed to ease regulations on bug sprays and other chemicals (go figure). Yet, he never sought the spotlight. And for good reason. DeLay watched attentively as a more politically palatable Republican leader, former House Speaker Newt Gingrich, whom DeLay believed to be too gentle with Democrats, too liberal on the issues, and too cozy with reporters, was destroyed—vampire-style—by the light of public scrutiny.

Generally politicians crave titles. But not DeLay. After the demise of Gingrich, the terrible Texan handed the House Speakership to his lamentable lieutenant, former high school wrestling coach Dennis Hastert. Through two Congresses, Hastert has maintained the charade of leadership while inevitably deferring to DeLay. Comfortably ensconced in the third tier of the Republican Congressional leadership, DeLay pretty much runs the Capitol. He has successfully blocked campaign finance reforms that might limit the activities of his multi-million-dollar political operation and has promoted an agenda so extreme that *New York Times* columnist Bob Herbert once argued: "Anyone trying to move further to the right than Tom DeLay is in danger of falling into the void."

> "Anyone trying to move further to the right than Tom DeLay is in danger of falling into the void"
>
> —BOB HERBERT

The man Republicans quietly refer to as their party's "crazy aunt in the basement."

☞ **Bipartisanship:** "Fuck that, it's time for all-out war."

☞ **The Environmental Protection Agency:** "the Gestapo of government."

☞ **Corporate sweatshops:** "a free-market success."

☞ **International affairs:** "The Serbian people are rallying around [Slobodan Milosevic] like never before."

☞ **The Nobel Prize committee:** "Swedish environmental extremists."

☞ **Campaign finance reform:** "Money is not the root of all evil in politics. In fact, money is the lifeblood of politics."

☞ **The massacre of students and teachers at Columbine High School:** Here, the National Rifle Association and National Right-to-Life 100-percenter combined his pro-gun and anti-abortion passions to place the blame for the shootings squarely on birth control, declaring that, "We have sterilized and contracepted our families down to sizes that the children we do have are so spoiled with material things that they come to equate the receiving of the material with love." For good measure, he targeted science for its share of the blame: "Our school systems teach the children they are nothing but glorified apes who are evolutionized out of some primordial soup of mud."

DeLay's whip position makes him the Republican majority's House Hall Monitor. DeLay is an enforcer of discipline who relishes the role—nicknaming himself "the Hammer," displaying bullwhips on his office wall, and placing a regularly updated list of the amounts key interest groups have contributed to Republican campaigns next to the Bible on his desk. DeLay declares with the snarl of a dominatrix in politician drag, "Politics is about rewards and punishments, about consequences and cause and effect."

If reporters had ever gone in serious search of the "vast right-wing conspiracy" Hillary Clinton discussed when DeLay was orchestrating the impeachment of her husband, there would have been no better place to begin the hunt than in the thicket of organizations *U.S. News and World Report* refers to as "DeLay Inc." That's the unofficial title given the interlocking network of organizations that range from non-profit groups benignly named the U.S. Family Network and Americans for Economic Growth to political action committees such as Americans for a Republican Majority. With its intricate webs of political fund-raising, communication, and "education" initiatives—all linked to the man who effectively controls whether major legislation is passed by the U.S. House of Representatives—it came as no surprise that DeLay Inc. was the subject of broad calls in 2000 for an investigation under the Racketeer Influenced and Corrupt Organizations (RICO) Act. DeLay laughed off the charges with the bravado of a man not unfamiliar with racketeering statutes. "First of all, I am not stupid," bragged DeLay. "Every step I take is monitored by lawyers."

Needless to say, the organizers of George W. Bush's presidential campaign did not seek to associate their candidate closely with the governor's fellow Texan. "Bush is not Tom DeLay," declared Mark McKinnon, the presidential candidate's media adviser, early on. Throughout the campaign, aides to the two men meticulously assured

> "Every step I take is monitored by lawyers"
>
> —TOM DELAY

What's With DeLay Inc.?

SCOTT HATCH
(FORMER DeLAY AIDE, REPUBLICAN
CONGRESSIONAL CAMPAIGN
COMMITTEE EXECUTIVE DIRECTOR):
"DeLay Incorporated is one of
the most savvy, aggressive politi-
cal teams ever built."

NORM ORNSTEIN
(AMERICAN ENTERPRISE INSTITUTE):
"[Republicans] needed a
rottweiler. And there aren't
many members who have
[DeLay's] kind of toughness."

**U.S. REPRESENTATIVE
PETER DEUTSCH:**
"A group of out-of-state, paid
political operatives came to
south Florida in an attempt to
stop countywide recounts. They
crossed state lines and intimidated the counting in a federal election, which is a violation of the
Voting Rights Act."

that they were not photographed together—to such an extent that Representative Martin Frost (D-Tex.) gleefully remarked to the *Dallas Morning News* that the Republican presidential candidate feared being linked with his own party's congressional leadership. Bush seemed to confirm the view during a 1999 budget standoff when he charged that DeLay's wing of the GOP was seeking to "balance their budget on the backs of the poor." Never one to back down from a fight, DeLay fired back: "It's obvious Mr. Bush needs a little education on how Congress works."

Bush and DeLay had never been close—Texas maintains a healthy enough class system to assure that oil company executives, even failed oil company executives, do not have to associate with "pest control executives," as DeLay's precongressional occupation is listed in *Congressional Quarterly*. Bush never forgave or forgot DeLay's scorched-earth campaign to block the 1990 tax increase backed by then–president George "No New Taxes" Bush. That was a career-defining crusade for DeLay, cinching the relatively new congressman's reputation as the craziest of the House's crazy-ass Republicans. DeLay's machinations handed Pat Buchanan an issue he would use to skewer Daddy Bush in the 1992 New Hampshire primary. Years later, DeLay worried that Bush Jr. would turn out to be his father's son—a Milquetoast Republican who would crack when the Holy War got hot.

Though DeLay was the most powerful Texan on the national political scene throughout Bush's tenure as Texas governor, the congressman admitted that the two had "never had dinner. We aren't social friends."

Once Bush had secured the Republican nomination, however, there was never any question of DeLay's loyalty—not to Bush but to the cause of denying Democrats the hold on the White House that had prevented implementation of the House Republican's fundamentalist regimen. At the start of the 2000 campaign season, DeLay told a Heritage Foundation confab, "Our cause—the defense of our values—has never changed; we lack only a united conservative front that can guide a cause to victory. And that means a Republican president working with a Republican Congress."

At the 2000 Texas state Republican Convention in Houston, where DeLay's speech followed a prayer rally at which the state's history was "honored" by the display of a Confederate flag, the House whip went biblical—declaring a jihad in which Republicans must not suffer defeat by "a media who despises our beliefs, by a Hollywood elite that detests our values, and certainly not by a Democratic vice president who demeans our very notion of decency." The Hammer was coming down on Al Gore's candidacy, and DeLay would not let up until the Gore campaign was dead. "Mr. Gore," DeLay told Houston's hooting Republicans, "we will not surrender—not today, not tomorrow, not ever."

With DeLay there to rally the troops, George W. Bush skipped his home-state party convention that year. However, a videotape of the governor was shown. In it, ironically, he told delegates he was out of Texas because he was campaigning in the state that already had come to be identified as a critical battleground in the 2000 campaign: Florida. Bush quipped, "We better carry Florida this year, or my little brother, Jeb, Florida's governor, will have some explaining to do."

The House whip went biblical—declaring a jihad in which Republicans must not suffer defeat

"I've never been able to understand that 'turn-the-other-cheek' stuff."

—Tom DeLay on the mysteries of Christianity

Tom DeLay's worst fears about the Milquetoast Bushes were threatening to be realized

Jeb Bush ended up having some explaining to do. Instead of sweeping Florida for his brother November 7, Jeb and the Florida Republican Party found themselves bogged down in a postelection swamp that was infested with uncounted ballots all but certain to hand the presidency to Gore. And Jeb, who had already blown the election, seemed to be blowing the recount. Tom DeLay's worst fears about the Milquetoast Bushes were threatening to be realized. But if the Bush family did not have what it took to secure the White House, DeLay did.

For the first 10 days after the November 7 election, the Bush team out of Austin was in charge of the public fight for Florida, as former secretary of state James Baker used procedural ploys to block the Gore campaign's efforts to secure a hand recount of ballots in key counties. But behind the scenes, DeLay and his minions prepared and distributed a two-page memo to Republican House members and their aides, detailing how Congress could overturn a recount that went Gore's way. Echoing DeLay's "impeachment book"—an outline of how the House would impeach Bill Clinton that DeLay used as a roadmap during the 1998 Monica mess—the memo explained that if a Florida recount awarded the state's 25 electoral votes to Gore, House and Senate Republicans could use ancient statutes to reject those electors and ultimately secure a victory for Bush. According to the *Dallas Morning News,* "The memo included a citation from the U.S. code that says the House and Senate 'concurrently may reject the vote or votes if they consider them to be tainted.' DeLay would not answer questions

Tom "Quackers" DeLay

Washington, D.C., is full of odd ducks, but the quackiest by far is also the most powerful: Tom DeLay.

This former pest exterminator from Sugar Land is not merely eaten up with right-wing ideology, he's messianic in his drive to foist it on the rest of us. How far out is Tom? He thinks Bush is a liberal and that middle-of-the-road Democrats are socialists. He thinks it was wrong to ban DDT, that the minimum wage should be eliminated, that clean-air and clean-water laws should be repealed, that worker-safety laws should be scrapped, and that corporate America must be liberated from regulations that protect consumers and workers.

Tom sees politics as a "battle for souls." DeLay recently told the *Washington Post* that he seeks to build a "God-centered" nation whose government will promote prayer and worship. His godly government limits the rights of homosexuals, curbs contraception, ends the separation of church and state, outlaws abortion, and posts the Ten Commandments in every public school.

Asked about the majority of citizens who would feel somewhere between uncomfortable and terrified by his plan to mold our government to the dictates of his religion, DeLay sighed sadly and told the *Post*: "When faced with the truth, the truth hurts . . . . People hate the messenger. That's why they killed Christ."

Whoa, Tom—I think you've got your halo a little too tight! It would be one thing if such quackiness was coming from just another lawmaker, but DeLay is the most powerful man in Congress, serving as party whip and controlling a vast network of fundraising entities and extremist political operations. George Bush says he wants to put a compassionate face on the GOP, but Tom DeLay is the real face of Republican power. **—Jim Hightower**

National radio commentator, writer, public speaker, and author of If the Gods Had Meant Us to Vote They Would Have Given Us Candidates, *Jim Hightower has spent three decades battling the Powers That Be on behalf of the Powers That Ought To Be— consumers, working families, environmentalists, small businesses, and just-plain-folks.*

about the memo, but his aide Jonathan Baron wrapped the document in a good-government cloak, saying, 'Mr. DeLay is committed to ensuring the Constitution is followed.'" Of course, DeLay's constitutional commitment did not extend to protecting Gore's rights or those of the Florida voters who backed the Democrat; Laura Nichols, an aide to House Minority Leader Richard Gephardt, said of the DeLay memo: "I guarantee if Bush wins we will not be hearing [Republicans talking about the authority of Congress to overturn the Florida count]." (Indeed, when members of the Congressional Black Caucus sought in January to employ portions of the strategy DeLay outlined in his memo, as part of a last-ditch attempt to open a debate over the Florida fiasco, members of the whip's team joined other top Republicans in ridiculing the initiative.)

As the Florida fight geared up, DeLay became increasingly agitated. A frequent critic of the courts, he condemned the Florida Supreme Court's November 17 ruling that counties should be allowed time to review disputed ballots, calling the decision "radical judicial activism" and "a breach of the most basic principles of jurisprudence." The man who weeks later would hail the U.S. Supreme Court's decision to end all recounts, declared this night that "unrestrained judicial power endangers representative democracy."

About this time, DeLay began participating in daily conference calls with top Bush aides in Austin, including chief campaign strategist Karl Rove and communications director Karen Hughes. And DeLay Inc. swung into full campaign mode. ARMPAC's "GOP Today" web site ramped up the rhetoric, with DeLay urging visitors to read "war room" missives from right-wing commentator David Horowitz. Those raw-meat reports featured headlines such as "The Democrats' Racial Arsonists Spearhead an Attempted Coup D'etat" and "Al Gore Demonstrates Why He Is Not Fit to Be President." One battle bulletin

As the Florida fight geared up, DeLay became increasingly agitated

appearing beneath the heading, "By David Horowitz—brought to you by Tom DeLay," read, "[Al Gore] unleashed the dogs of political war on Palm Beach County. He allowed the (Jesse) Jackson arsonists to rush in to inflame the passions of social hysteria, to recklessly sow bitter doubts about the process itself that no one can now allay. He allowed the chief of his campaign to suggest that the Constitution be overthrown so that the popular vote would prevail—because that was 'morally' more right than letting the electoral college decide. He launched a partisan and enormously dangerous campaign to undermine the very process that keeps the nation united, and that alone can make the next administration a government of us all. In launching this destructive action, Al Gore poured the corrosive acid of suspicion and distrust on an already fraying body politic, and showed in one reckless decision during a moment of crisis, that he is not fit to be president of these United States."

A Republican riot might well be the last hope for the fast-sinking Bush campaign

The targeting of Jackson's role in south Florida protests was part of an intentional Republican initiative to obscure the fact that the streets of Palm Beach, Broward, and Miami-Dade County communities were filled with local voters, most of them carrying hand-lettered signs that called for a full recount. The spin was relentless. Republican commentators such as Mary Matalin, who would soon trade her "analyst" gig on television news programs for a job with the Bush-Cheney administration, returned again and again to the charge that Jackson was leading crews of "rent-a-rioters." But even as Republican operatives were denouncing Jackson and others for stirring sentiments in Florida, they were coming to the conclusion that a Republican riot might well be the last hope for the fast-sinking Bush campaign. This was a job for DeLay Inc. And thus, for all the talk of Jackson and Democratic minions, the real *agent provocateurs* turned out to be Republican "rent-a-rioters" who regularly collected their paychecks from DeLay Inc. and the GOP congressional offices the whip whipped into action.

> "You're going to think I'm crazy, but I didn't see this as a tie election."
>
> —Tom DeLay on the Bush-Gore contest in Florida

On November 21, the Florida Supreme Court set a tight yet seemingly workable schedule for completing the recount by November 26, a Sunday. If Gore could make up an official deficit of 930 votes over those five days, he would have his claim to Florida's electoral votes and the presidency.

DeLay went ballistic, denouncing the Florida Court's ruling as "a blatant and extraordinary abuse of judicial power." The various DeLay Inc. web sites—most of them rigorously bookmarked by true-believing GOP congressional aides—were flashing with pronouncements from the congressman to the effect that, "With this decision, a collection of liberal activists has arbitrarily swept away thoughtfully designed statutes ensuring free and fair elections and replaced them with their own political opinions."

Of course, no serious scholar of election law or practices doubted the authority of a state court to extend a certification deadline until the ballots in a close election had been reviewed. That is standard procedure nationwide—even in Texas, where DeLay's own Republican Party had used the courts to extend vote-counting deadlines.

But that did not stop the Hammer from sending a none-too-subtle call to action: "I hope this misguided ruling will be vigorously challenged," ended a November 21 DeLay missive.

As DeLay well knew, the most vigorous challenge of the entire 36-day Florida fight was already in the works. Indeed, DeLay Inc. operatives were already in the air, headed for the Holy War.

By the time the sun dawned over south Florida on Wednesday,

November 22, Broward County had completed a hand recount of 609 precincts, which showed a net gain of 106 votes for Gore. Palm Beach County continued to plod forward with a recount that had yielded a modest gain for Gore. But the real action was in the Stephen P. Clark Government Center in the heart of Miami, where the three-member Miami-Dade County Canvassing Board appeared to be sitting atop a Gore gold mine. Miami-Dade officials had wanted to review all 653,963 ballots cast by the county's voters, but the deadline forced a decision to conduct a manual recount of only the 10,750 ballots on which machines had not been able to determine the choice of the voter. Already, that recount had yielded a net gain for Gore of 157 votes.

The review of ballots being conducted by Miami-Dade County Supervisor of Elections David Leahy and County Judges Lawrence King and Myriam Lehr was a tedious process involving the visual examination of each punch card for evidence of a break in the paper or deep indentation that, while undetectable by a scanning machine, would indicate a clear preference to the human eye. The task was made more difficult by the press of reporters, lawyers, official election observers from both the Bush and Gore camps, and a rapidly growing crowd of raucous young people in business suits.

White, blond, and predominantly preppy, the crew of young men and a few women stood out in a county where Cuban and Haitian immigrants,

"DELAYED" REACTION

GEORGE W. BUSH:
"Well, DeLay's a good friend of mine. As you know, we're both Texans. I've known him a long time. I like him and respect him and I hope I'm working with him. I hope I'm working with him. I hope I win."

COKIE ROBERTS:
"And one of the things that Republicans in Congress are saying is that they really need to let George Bush become the face of the party, that that is the best thing that can happen to them, because they don't want Tom DeLay particularly to be the face of the party, and they're still smarting over Newt Gingrich."

BOB HERBERT (THE NEW YORK TIMES): "Tom DeLay spent many long months hiding in the tall grass and chuckling while George W. Bush traveled the country trying to spread the fiction of compassionate conservatism."

From **ARIANNA HUFFINGTON**'s list of gifts for her favorite—and not so favorite—public figures:
Tom DeLay's "Riotous" Staffers: Acting classes with GOP Repertory members Charlton Heston and Bo Derek, so that next time they can pull off a more believable "idealistic young Republicans" routine.

African Americans, and elderly Jews dominate the demographics. "There were no guayaberas," a local told veteran Miami reporter John Lantigua, noting that despite the heat none of the rabble-rousers wore the traditional open shirt of Miami Cubans. "This crowd looked tweedy. They were from out of town." Indeed, with their ears glued to cell phones and their distinctly un-Miami southern accents, the crowd resembled nothing so much as a pack of renegade Republican congressional aides and lobbyists—the sort of folks who cluster in the Washington offices of Tom DeLay and his congressional and corporate allies.

And so they were, though the canvassing board, the Gore observers, and most of the media were unaware of it at the time.

On Wednesday morning, the members of the board of canvassers decided that, if they were going to complete the review of more than 10,000 ballots by Sunday, they would have to move to a smaller and, they hoped, quieter room near the computerized scanning machines on the nineteenth floor of the Clark Building. Bush and Gore observers would still be permitted to monitor the count, as would a media pool consisting of reporters who would then pass information on to the broader pack.

On this simple attempt at efficiency turned the fate of the recount, and the presidency. The mysterious crowd of suit-and-tie Republicans appeared to be looking for direction to Representative John Sweeney (R-N.Y.), a former executive director of the New York State Republican Party, who had shown up in Florida to derail the Miami-Dade recount. Who might have invited Sweeney down to Miami? Well, let's speculate:

☞ Sweeney made his first race for public office in 1998 and won, with the help of a check for $5,000 from Tom DeLay's leadership PAC, Americans for a Republican Majority.

REPUBLICAN RIOT, 2000

Media reports described how a "riot" stopped the Miami-Dade recounts on November 22, 2000. Al Kamen's "In the Loop" column in the *Washington Post* of December 6, 2000 idenified the "penny-loafer protesters" as:

1. **TOM PYLE**, policy analyst, office of House Majority Whip Tom DeLay (R-Tex.).

2. **GARRY MALPHRUS**, majority chief counsel and staff director, House Judiciary subcommittee on criminal justice.

3. **RORY COOPER**, political division staff member at the National Republican Congressional Committee.

4. **KEVIN SMITH**, former House Republican conference analyst and more recently of Voter.com.

5. **STEVEN BROPHY**, former aide to Senator Fred D. Thompson (R-Tenn.), now working at the consulting firm KPMG.

6. **MATT SCHLAPP**, former chief of staff for Representative Todd Tiahrt (R-Kan.), then on the Bush campaign staff in Austin.

7. **ROGER MORSE**, aide to Representative Van Hilleary (R-Tenn.).

8. **DUANE GIBSON**, aide to Chairman Don Young (R-Alaska) of the House Resources Committee.

9. **CHUCK ROYAL**, legislative assistant to Representative Jim DeMint (R-S.C.).

10. **LAYNA MCCONKEY**, former legislative assistant to former Representative Jim Ross Lightfoot (R-Iowa), then at Steelman Health Strategies.

☞ Sweeney spent much of his first term taking potshots at Hillary Clinton—for instance, he sponsored an amendment to a campaign finance reform bill designed to force the First Lady to reimburse the federal government for the cost of military planes she was required to travel in at the behest of the Secret Service. *USA Today* reported an interesting footnote: "Sweeney's amendment was drafted in cooperation with House Majority Whip Tom DeLay, R-Texas."

☞ Sweeney had recently landed a plumb assignment on the powerful House Appropriations Committee with the approval and support of another committee member, Tom DeLay.

Was Sweeney in Florida at DeLay's behest? Sweeney wasn't saying, and neither was the Hammer. But Representative Sherrod Brown (D-Ohio), a former Ohio Secretary of State who visited Florida to observe the recount, had no doubts about what he saw. "It was a classic whip operation. The Republicans were running it just like they do a big vote in Congress," said Brown, a House veteran. "Anybody who didn't see the DeLay imprint on this one wasn't looking."

There was no denying the Hammer-like effect of Sweeney's presence. When word came that the board of canvassers had made a move intended to speed up the count, Sweeney ordered his Brooks Brothers Battalion into action. What were they to do? "Shut it down," Sweeney cried.

Television and still photographers captured the scene that followed. Dozens of neatly attired, carefully coiffed "radicals" stormed through the hallways of the Clark Building, punching and kicking local Democrats, trampling people, and ultimately crowding into a narrow hallway outside the glass doors of the office of the Miami-Dade supervisor of elections. "The Republicans are clearly trying to throw an obstacle into . . . determining the will of the voters," warned state senator Debbie Wasserman Schultz (D-Davie). "They are hell bent on producing the desired outcome that they want." Packs of the protesters broke off to chase Democrats out of the building. One group went after Miami-Dade County Democratic Party chair Joe Geller, whom they accused of stealing a contested ballot. Geller, who was simply examining a sample ballot, recalls, "Suddenly, I was surrounded by a scream-

ing, shoving, insane crowd, shouting that I had done something that I hadn't done. [There were] people grabbing at me and my clothes and there was almost no security. I couldn't believe these people weren't arrested."

Geller was finally escorted to safety by local police. But by then the crowd outside the doors to the elections office had become a teeming mosh pit of political grievances. "Stop the count!" they screamed as their leaders banged fists on the glass. "Stop the fraud!" Rumors came from the mob that a thousand angry Cuban Americans were massing outside the building to storm it—no idle threat in Miami, a town still raw with tension from the Elian Gonzalez clashes of earlier in the year.

The Cubans never showed. (For all the talk of how the Clinton administration's order to remove six-year-old Elian from the home of his Miami relatives and return him to his Cuban father would destroy Gore in Miami-Dade, the Democrat ended up carrying the county by a handsome 53 to 46 margin.) But the members of the canvassing board weren't going to wait around for more trouble.

After a team of sheriff's deputies restored order, the three judges asked for a police escort to return them to the larger recounting room they had exited only a short time earlier. There, they voted unanimously to end their recount. Under the circumstances, the canvassers said, they could not possibly complete an accurate recount in time to meet the Sunday deadline. Thus, the thousands of ballots that machines had not counted would not be reviewed. The 157 additional Gore votes that already had been discovered in the Miami-Dade recount were discarded. Vote totals from Florida's most populous county would revert to the pre-recount figures.

The Izod insurgents greeted the decision with chants of "President Bush."

David Leahy, the supervisor of elections, was reported by the *New York Times* as saying that canvassing board members had been intimidated by the rioters. "This was perceived as not being an open and fair process," he said of the recount. "That weighed heavy on our minds."

Later, perhaps recognizing that his words could create the basis for a legal challenge to the board's decision, Leahy denied that the board was intimidated, claiming that the tight recount schedule was the only factor the board considered. Few believed him. "The canvassing board bowed under pressure," declared Representative Carrie Meek (D-Fla.), who represents much of Miami in Congress.

Still, the courts did not immediately order the canvassing board back to the counting tables. The Bush campaign's legal and public-relations teams jumped into action to defend the Miami-Dade decision, and on the Wednesday evening before Thanksgiving, Murray Greenberg, a lawyer for the canvassing board, announced that a Florida appeals court had turned down the Gore campaign's request to restart the count.

"The canvassing board bowed under pressure"

—U.S. REPRESENTATIVE CARRIE MEEK

That night and throughout the Thanksgiving weekend, media reports portrayed the "riot" as a grassroots rebellion. CNN kept running clips of Geller being chased through the Clark Building. Lucianne Goldberg, who had spun a peripheral role in the Monica Lewinsky mess into steady work as a right-wing commentator, described "angry Republicans in high rampage," while the conservative NewsMax.com web site hailed "grassroots GOP outrage." Most newspapers simply reported, as the *Los Angeles Times* did, that "a horde of shouting, shoving protesters—many wearing suits—stormed an upper floor of a skyscraper [in Miami]. An elections department receptionist fled in panic as angry Republicans pounded on the door." The "Say What?" Award went to the *New York Times,* which portrayed the protest as having been organized by local Republicans and made up of "staunchly Republican Cuban-Americans" concerned that "the recount was biased against Hispanics."

While accurate information slipped out piecemeal during the days following the Republican riot, no major newspaper or television network moved during the critical period before the Sunday certification of the statewide recount to take a serious look at the photographs of the protesters who had mounted the Miami-Dade demonstration. If they had, they would have found that local faces, Cuban or otherwise, were in short supply. None bothered to aggressively investigate, at the point when it really mattered, the assertion by Democratic Party chair Geller that "this was not a Miami moment. It was outsiders, Hitler youth, sent in by Republicans to intimidate the election officials."

And not just any outsiders.

Right up there at the front of one of the most dramatic photographs of the rioters pushing toward the door of the elections office was none other than Tom Pyle, a top policy analyst in the office of Tom DeLay. DeLay's office would later claim that Pyle was "on vacation" in Miami

> "It was outsiders, Hitler youth, sent in by Republicans to intimidate the election officials"
>
> —MIAMI POLITICO JOSEPH GELLER

that day. Also taking in some sun on the Clark Building's nineteenth floor was Mike Murphy, a key player at ARMPAC, DeLay's political action committee. As columnist Bob Herbert noted after the full details of the riot began to come out, it was now obvious that DeLay and his minions had decided "to go to the mattresses."

Among those photographed in the bang-on-the-door incident were aides to present or former Republican representatives Don Young (R-Ark.), Van Hilleary (R-Tenn.), Todd Tiahrt (R-Kans.), Jim DeMint (R-S.C.), and Jim Lightfoot (R-Iowa), as well as the chief counsel for the House Judiciary Subcommittee on Criminal Justice, a member of the political staff for the National Republican Congressional Committee, and representatives of various Republican-friendly lobbying firms. They all had Washington-area addresses. All were "vacationing"—or as the *Wall Street Journal* would later explain, "[taking] advantage of liberal congressional workplace rules that allow them to jump from government jobs to political tasks at a moment's notice by declaring themselves to be on vacation or temporary leave." It turns out that close to 200 congressional staffers and Washington Republican stalwarts made the all-expense-paid trip to Florida, stayed in Hilton and Sheraton Hotels on the beachfront, and collected "walking around money" from Republican operatives. They were dispatched across south Florida with partisan mischief in mind—indeed, on the Sunday after the Miami-Dade riot, a group of the khaki commandos were seen confronting the Reverend Al Sharpton in West Palm Beach. Ironically, the congressional aides from Washington were yelling, "Go home!" at the preacher. "All we are doing is rallying and protesting. We are blowing the Democrats away," one protester said during the pivotal week. When *Journal* reporters finally began to investigate—long after the Miami-Dade count had been shut down— they said they found that "there has been an air of mystery to the operation." Memos were slipped under hotel-room doors late each night,

Close to 200 congressional staffers and Washington Republican stalwarts made the all-expense-paid trip to Florida

instructing the wrecking crews where to show up next. "To tell you the truth, nobody knows who is calling the shots," claimed one protester.

But, after reviewing photographs and identifications of protesters published in Al Kamen's *Washington Post* politics column, House Minority Leader Dick Gephardt (D-Mo.) managed to figure out what the Republican rampager claimed he could not. "Republican whip Tom DeLay dispatched staffers to Florida, not to observe the count, but to disrupt it," Gephardt declared.

In a blatant acknowledgment of the decisive role they had played, the Brooks Brothers Battalion did what comes "naturally" for twenty-somethings "on vacation." They got down with Wayne Newton. On Thanksgiving night, at the ritzy Hyatt on Pier 66 in Fort Lauderdale, the food was free, as were the drinks. Vegas lounge singer Newton—who had appeared in Austin at Bush's November 7 "victory party that wasn't" flew in to sing. The singer performed a "fresh" rendition of his 1960s hit, "Danke Schoen"—that's German for "thank you." The highlights of the Thanksgiving party were phone calls from a pair of grateful candidates: George W. Bush phoning in from Texas and Dick Cheney from the hospital bed where he was recovering from bypass surgery. Both joked about the Miami-Dade riot and the shutdown of the count that followed.

Bush and Cheney had reason to thank the 150 or so imported insurrectionists. As the clock ticked down toward the 5:00 P.M. Sunday deadline for certification of the recount, it became clear that the Gore campaign would fall just short of surmounting Bush's "lead." Sure, Secretary of State Harris helped a bit, by allowing one county to throw out recount figures that favored Gore and by denying Palm Beach County a brief extension to finish its count. But nothing smoothed Harris's task of certifying a Bush win so much as the absence of any new numbers from Florida's most populous county, Miami-Dade.

When the 5:00 P.M. deadline passed, Harris certified Bush's victory over Gore by 537 votes at a ceremony that one observer described as featuring "all the fanfare of an international treaty signing." Moments later, Bush leaped before cameras in Texas to announce, "The election was close, but tonight after a count, a recount, and yet another manual recount, Secretary Cheney and I are honored and humbled to have won the state of Florida, which gives us the needed electoral votes to win the election. We will therefore undertake the responsibility of preparing to serve as America's next president and vice president."

For good measure, Bush warned Gore not to object: "If the vice president chooses to go forward, he is filing a contest to the outcome of the election, and that is not the best route for America." Former secretary of state James Baker, Bush's pointman in Florida, was more blunt. "At some point, there must be closure. At some point, the law must prevail and the lawyers must go home," Baker said. "We have reached that point."

But Baker could not rival the fierce language of a short missive dispatched from the Washington office of Tom DeLay: "It is now clear that no number of recounts, if lawful, will change the outcome of this presidential contest. For this reason, continued litigation by Mr. Gore

Bush and Cheney called to thank the Izod Insurgents

can only be viewed as an abuse of the legal system and an attempt to defy our constitutional system of government."

As it happened, Democratic appeals continued through the courts, finally securing a Florida Supreme Court order to finish the Miami-Dade recount. DeLay blew. "This judicial aggression must not stand," he declared. This time, Democrats recognized that when DeLay spoke on such matters, he was not simply expressing an opinion—but rather an order. House Minority Leader Gephardt held a press conference to say, "I call on [DeLay], on all leaders on both sides, not to engage in improper tactics. This election should be settled by counting the ballots, not by intimidating the counters. If [the Republican riot in Miami-Dade] had not happened, the votes would already be counted today. The adherents of Governor Bush have no right to decry the chaos they have sought to create."

DeLay would not need to act this time. A higher power was about to intervene.

When the count was halted again by the U.S. Supreme Court, DeLay was bouncing like a Texas jackrabbit.

After the Court handed the election to Bush, DeLay chirped, "This is something I've been working on for 22 years. I mean, we got it."

This time, DeLay was not complaining about judicial aggression. Rather, he was claiming a mandate—not for George W. Bush but for his personal agenda. "You're going to think I'm crazy, but I didn't see this as a tie election. We have the House, we have the Senate, we have the White House, which means we have the agenda."

Was DeLay going overboard with all that "we" talk? George W. Bush didn't object. After years of sparring with his fellow Texan, Bush had taken a clear message away from Florida: It helps to have the Hammer bang things into place.

"If [the Republican riot] had not happened, the votes would already be counted today"

—HOUSE MINORITY LEADER RICHARD GEPHARDT

CHAPTER 7

Bushwhacked by the Better Brother

"I will deliver Florida to my brother."
—Jeb Bush, November 6, 2000

Every family has its secrets—the dark truths that they prefer to leave unspoken. And a family that places a former director of the Central Intelligence Agency at the head of its Thanksgiving table knows more than it should about unspoken history. But there is one Bush family secret that tops the list of no-go subject matter. It's not the exact price tag for bailing out brother Neil Bush in the Silverado Banking, Savings & Loan scandal of the 1980s. It's not even the question of whether that drunk driving arrest is the last entry on George W.'s police blotter. The most taboo of taboo topics at any gathering of the nation's reigning political dynasty is the identity of the Bush brother who was supposed to revenge Bush the Elder's 1992 defeat at the hands of William Jefferson Clinton.

Here's a hint: His name isn't George W.

As recently as 1994, George W. was well out of the running. With his history of drug and drinking problems, his repeated business fail-

George W. made Dan Quayle look presidential

ures, his slim familiarity with the English language, and his not-quite-Protestant work ethic, George W. made Dan Quayle look presidential. Even in Texas, where he settled after finishing his cheerleading duties at Andover and collecting a Skull and Bones membership card at Yale, W. had a reputation as a loser and a lightweight. Defeated for Congress in 1978, he settled into a routine of using his father's name to shake down investors in a series of progressively more ludicrous get-poor-quick oil-field schemes. George W. acknowledged his lack of political viability in 1989, when he told a reporter, "You know, I could run for governor but I'm basically a media creation. I've never done anything. I've worked for my dad. I worked in the oil business. But that's not the kind of profile you have to have to get elected to public office."

The star-quality Bush was W.'s younger, smarter, better-looking brother Jeb. John Ellis Bush (JEB) was always the Bush with presidential potential. Naturally easygoing, quick on his feet, and capable of stringing together full sentences in English and Spanish, Jeb was everything George W. was not. If Jeb was solid presidential timber, W. was, well, a shrub, as Texas journalist Molly Ivins so memorably dubbed him. The brothers were so differently abled—with Jeb such an obviously superior sibling—that it became the stuff of a "Saturday Night Live" comedy routines in which a concerned Al Gore discussed the fate of the nation with Jeb as a feral George W. played, catlike, with a ball of string. "You're a good man, Jeb," says Gore in the skit. To which Jeb replies, "Only in comparison."

During the 2000 campaign, after the Texas governor had gained the unanimous nomination of his party for president, a conscious effort was made by top Republicans to avoid the comparison by keeping brother Jeb under wraps. "Everybody was anxious for George to do his own thing," explained Florida Republican National Committeeman

Tom Slade, "and there was a level of sensitivity that they didn't want to overshadow him [with Jeb]."

That was wise politics, as Jeb so clearly seemed to have what George W. was lacking. An outstanding student who developed a lifelong interest in international affairs before finishing high school, Jeb graduated magna cum laude with a degree in Latin American Studies from the University of Texas; married the beautiful Mexican woman who was his high school pen pal; started his business career as a high-flying international banker in Caracas; relocated to Miami, where he established one of the most successful real estate development corporations in that 1980s boomtown; made his fortune; and entered the political arena. After chairing the Dade County Republican Party through a successful Republican presidential race (1984) and gubernatorial campaign (1986), he was appointed to serve as Florida's secretary of commerce—establishing him as the Reagan-Bush administration's most valued link to south Florida's politically potent and economically powerful Cuban-American community.

Even as George the Elder was seeking and winning the presidency in 1988, Jeb was being touted as "the next-generation Bush." He was, in the words of *U.S. News and World Report* political correspondent Roger Simon, "the brother that many had assumed would end up in the White House."

By 1994, the year in which the Bush brothers would become the first siblings since Nelson and Winthrop Rockefeller to seek the governorships of separate states in the same year, George W. was a largely unproven campaigner, and Texas was still tough political turf for Republicans—the party had won just two gubernatorial races since Reconstruction. His opponent would be Democratic governor Ann Richards, a sly fox known for skewering Bushes, as when she dismissed Bush the Elder as having been "born with a silver foot in his mouth."

"I'm basically a media creation. I've never done anything"

—GEORGE W. BUSH

Florida, on the other hand, appeared to be fertile ground for the GOP. With a record of voting Republican for president since the 1950s and for governor since the 1960s, the state's Republican Party has grown by leaps and bounds as conservative retirees from the north and Bush-backing Miami Cubans swelled its ranks. Democratic governor Lawton Chiles, who got his start in Florida politics when his Republican challenger was five years old, looked worn out next to the fresh young Jeb. Recalling the contests the Bush brothers entered in 1994, *Dallas Morning News* writer Todd J. Gillman, a veteran Bush watcher, remembered Jeb as "the more likely win." And with that Florida win, the assumption was that the Jeb Bush for President campaign would begin.

But in an unexpected twist, just as Florida gave the presidency to George W. Bush, it took the road up away from Jeb. While Bush family hangers-on poured money and tactical energy into shoring up George W.'s tenuous run in Texas, Jeb, who was thought to be more than capable of plotting his own course, ran so far to the right that he proclaimed himself a "head-banging conservative." Playing to Christian fundamentalists and the cold warriors in the Miami Cuban community to win a tough GOP primary, he ranted too long and too loud about how social programs represented a "silent march to socialism." Jeb picked as his running mate for lieutenant governor Tom Feeney, a Christian Coalition favorite who wanted Florida to sell "Choose Life" license tags as an anti-abortion statement. Feeney, who in 2000 would lead legislative efforts to simply declare George W. Bush the winner of the state's electoral votes, was described in that 1994 race by Chiles as "spooky" and by former Republican governor Claude Kirk as "a walking mental paraplegic." Even Jeb acknowledged that his running mate "may be a loose cannon." But that didn't prevent the gubernatorial nominee from parroting much of Feeney's extremism. Nor did it temper his arrogance—which was on overload, even for a Bush. Jeb told

African-American voters that they could expect "probably nothing" from a Bush administration. When an elderly woman said she appreciated the stance Bush's mother, Barbara, had taken in support of abortion rights, the candidate snapped, "Most people do. I don't." Chiles took to referring to Bush as "the radical."

Chiles, who had won four statewide election contests, proved to be a feistier contender than anyone expected. His campaign dug up records of shady financial deals involving Bush's real estate firm—including one loan default by Jeb and his partner that forced a Broward County savings and loan to collapse, but that, through the kind intervention of Reagan-era federal regulators, eventually allowed the Bush firm to sell the building for $8.7 million. Chiles got an unintended assist from Feeney, who said his gubernatorial running mate had been involved with "crooks and deadbeats." Chiles's television ads closed with the line, "We just can't trust Jeb Bush with our future."

The voters agreed. In the year of the greatest Republican sweep the nation had seen since the 1950s, Jeb Bush lost the governorship of Florida by 60,000 votes. His presidential prospects were dashed. But, conveniently for the White House–obsessed Bush family, they had an alternative candidate. Thanks to the sly machinations of Karl Rove, the House of Bush political fixer, George W. surfed the Republican tide over Ann Richards. In a political role reversal that was certainly as significant for the future of the Republican Party and the nation as another event that same evening—the takeover of the House of Representatives by Newt Gingrich's "Contract with America" crew—Jeb was off radar and George W. was suddenly a star.

The focus of Jeb's party and his family shifted immediately to George W., sending the Floridian into a tailspin that would eventually lead to his very-public conversion from the WASPy Episcopalianism of his parents to the Catholicism of his wife—whom he informed the

Jeb told African-American voters that they could expect "probably nothing" from a Bush administration

How many Bushes does it take to steal an election?

Miami Herald and all the world, was the only woman he had ever slept with. Jeb was putting his life on a dramatically different course. But that course did not lead him out of politics.

The Bush family does not accept defeat. Grandpa Prescott Bush ran for the Senate and lost in 1950 and then came back to claim his seat representing Connecticut in 1952. George the First ran for the U.S. Senate from Texas, lost, and then ran again. He put his name forward three times for the vice presidency and made a losing run at the presidency before finally riding what was left of Ronald Reagan's coattails into the White House. When Bill Clinton seized the presidency after Bush the Elder's first term, the family knew that Old George's running days were done. But they were determined to avenge the loss by bookending the Clinton presidency with another Bush administration.

Bottom line: the voters don't decide when a Bush's political career is done. The Bushes do.

Thus, the expectation from the night he conceded in 1994 was that Jeb would—like his father and grandfather before him—keep running until he got it right.

In 1998, the family had an added incentive to make sure Jeb secured the governorship of Florida, the fourth most populous state in the union, a political powerhouse that would send 80 delegates to the Republican National Convention in Philadelphia—more than any state except California, New York, and Texas. There was no better way to assure that those Florida delegates would be "Bush" backers than to put a Bush at the helm of the Sunshine State's Republican apparatus. More importantly, Florida had become a serious swing state that Republicans could no longer take for granted in November elections. A Reagan-Bush stronghold in 1980, 1984, 1988, and 1992, Florida and its 25 electoral votes had been plucked from the party's column by Bill Clinton in 1996. And Rove and the rest of the Bush political team were disturbed by a set of demographic trends that suggested Al Gore might be able to keep it Democratic.

So Jeb was running. And the Bush family would make sure that, this time, there would be no screwups on Election Day. A millionaire several times over, Jeb spent four years working full-time to remake his image as a right winger with a heart. Jeb joined community boards, he helped start a charter school in a tough African-American neighborhood of Miami, he hung out with migrant laborers in Immokalee. He still complained about taxes and government, but now he talked about the need for "acting on a sense of consciousness when you've seen the hurting and misery around you." He called this strange new political hybrid by a name that seemed a contradiction in terms at the time but that eventually would become his brother's mantra: "compassionate

Jeb spent four years working full-time to remake his image as a right winger with a heart

conservatism." And it paid rich dividends for him as the 1998 election approached. Several prominent African Americans, angered at being taken for granted by the Democratic Party, endorsed Jeb, helping him to pump up his percentage of the African-American vote from a dismal 6 percent in 1994 to a respectable 14 percent in 1998.

Chiles was term-limited out of the running. So it came as little surprise that a genuinely diversified base of support, a more mainstream message, piles of local and national campaign money—raised at fundraising events featuring Dad, Mom, and the governor of Texas—and a weak Democratic opponent would combine to make a Jeb win inevitable in 1998.

As soon as he hit the Governor's Mansion, Jeb got down to the business of securing the Florida franchise—and the presidency—for George W. In Tallahassee for his son's January 5, 1999, inauguration, Bush the Elder told reporters to "leave out the politics for a minute." But no one took him seriously. The Jeb-Bush-for-Governor campaign team was already converting into the Florida-George-W.-Bush-for-President campaign. Bush aides boasted on inaugural day that they would shake down wealthy Floridians for a full quarter of the $20 million the Texas governor would need to secure the GOP nomination. So hectic was the activity that the *Dallas Morning News* sent a presidential campaign reporter to Jeb's inaugural, for the simple reason that "the political ascension of the 45-year-old brother of Texas governor George W. Bush extends the reach of the Bush clan into two of the nation's most powerful states and could affect presidential politics and the Republican Party of the future." A political adviser to George W. was more blunt: Referring to Texas and Florida, he said, "If you can lock up the second- and fourth-largest states, that's a pretty good start toward 270 electoral votes."

"If you can lock up the second- and fourth-largest states, that's a pretty good start toward 270 electoral votes"

—A BUSH AIDE ON THE FAMILY'S CONTROL OF TEXAS AND FLORIDA

"Jeb Bush runs the Florida subsidiary of Bush, Inc."
—*New York Times* columnist Maureen Dowd

"It smacks of the old political machine approach."
—Florida comptroller Bob Milligan, a Republican,
on Jeb Bush's manipulation of the process
to win the state for his brother

Initially, it appeared that Jeb Bush would be nothing but an asset for his brother's campaign in Florida. Taking office in January 1999, he had only to keep his network of supporters and contributors energized until the campaign got started, quietly grease the official wheels so that they would spin in his brother's direction, and avoid polarizing the state in such a way that it would damage George W.'s chances. Had he succeeded on all three fronts, the state would have been labeled "Solid for Bush," the Democrats would have gone hunting elsewhere for their electoral votes, and Jeb Bush could have rested easy on the night of November 7, 2000.

But Jeb succeeded only in two of his responsibilities. And that meant he was sweating it November 7 and for five weeks thereafter.

Despite his obvious disappointment at how the family's presidential sweepstakes had turned out, Jeb had tried to deliver for George W. on Election Day. Indeed, considering the difficult family dynamics and the dubious qualifications of the candidate, Jeb did wonders:

☞ A skilled backroom pol who played a far more critical role than brother George W. in their father's 1980, 1988, and 1992 presidential campaigns, and who knew his way around the intricacies of Florida local politics as a former Republican county chairman, Jeb Bush well understood that depressing the vote from communities that were unlikely to support his brother was essential. The Jeb Bush administration refused requests for funding to update voting machines, expand voter education, and otherwise extend the franchise to all citizens in a state with an agonizing history of democratic denial. At the same time, the governor, along with Secretary of State Katherine Harris, agreed to foot the bill for a multi-million-dollar "voter purge" initiative, designed to quietly remove tens of thousands of likely Democratic voters from the polling lists. Using a law written by segregationists in the post–Civil War years to prevent African Americans from exercising the franchise, Bush and Harris spent roughly 4 million in taxpayer dollars to conduct the most aggressive review of election rolls ever initiated by a state government. The purge (as described in chapter 2) turned into one of the most effective assaults on minority voter participation since the post–Reconstruction era of the late nineteenth century. By the time the purge was done, fully 31 percent of Florida's African-American adult males were barred from voting.

31 percent of Florida's African-American adult males were barred from voting

To this day, Bush and his allies defend the purge as a legitimate removal of unqualified voters. "In fact," argues Gregory Palast, the investigative reporter for *The Observer* of London who did so much to expose the purge, "only a fraction were ex-cons. Most were simply guilty of being African American." Will Jeb Bush ever be called to account for the sort of actions that landed a previous generation of southern governors on the permanent dishonor roll? Probably not. When he testified before U.S. Civil Rights Commission hearings on the matter, the hands-on governor suddenly drew a blank. The commission determined that Bush, Harris, and their aides had engaged in "overzealous efforts" to purge the election rolls. Recognizing the absurdity of Jeb's sudden ignorance, commission chair Mary Frances Berry was being polite when she said, "We know there were barriers to people voting. What we don't know is whether those barriers were the result of discrimination or knuckleheadedness." Here's a clue: Jeb Bush is seldom identified as a knucklehead.

☞ A master fund-raiser, Jeb turned the Sunshine State into a prime source of George-W.-Bush-for-President campaign cash in an operation the *Dallas Morning News* referred to as "Hurricane Bush," because it seemed to sweep up every dollar in its path. A four-city Jeb and George fund-raising swing across the state in June 1999 collected $2 million for the presidential campaign. On that trip, George W. said of his little brother: "It helps to have friends in high places." According to Federal Election Commission documents, contributions of more than $200 from Florida givers to the Bush presidential campaign totaled $5,762,877—the third highest state total after Texas and California. Of 214 "Pioneers"—wealthy and powerful Republicans who committed early on to collect $100,000 each in contributions to the Bush campaign—20 were Floridians. (Only Texas was home to more Pioneers, and Florida's 20 dwarfed the 12 from California and 6 from New York.) Though they were raising money for George W. Bush, most of the Pioneers from Florida were Jeb acolytes. Many were old business associates from the red-hot south Florida real estate industry in which the governor had made his personal fortune; others were Bush appointees to the State Board of Regents and the

Florida Fish and Wildlife Conservation Committee, still others were executives of transportation and agribusiness firms with substantial holdings in Florida—and thus a genuine interest in maintaining good relations with the governor. Almost all used unregulated "soft-money" loopholes to give far more than the legal limit to advance Republican campaign prospects in 2000. For instance, Jeb Bush pal H. Gary Morse slipped a $100,000 soft-money check into the Republican National Committee's collection plate, and Miami Dolphins owner H. Wayne Huizenga's holding company pumped $522,370 into various GOP soft-money funds.

☞ An able strategist, Jeb dumbed himself down and edged out of the picture just enough to make his brother look good, explaining, "I'm his brother, so I have to be a bit more careful about how I help. Because of the comparisons that might not help George in some cases." What comparisons? Language skills? Looks? Popular appeal? Political savvy? Jeb wouldn't say, but everyone knew the answer: All of these and more. When *Wall Street Journal* columnist Paul Gigot said as much during the run-up to the 2000 campaign, Jeb remonstrated the conservative commentator for going off message. "I don't like the stories that are flattering me to make my brother look bad," Jeb cautioned.

At the same time, Jeb didn't mind using his position to make his brother look good. In a state with a large retired military population that was sympathetic to Republican John McCain's presidential candidacy, Jeb moved early and unequivocally to secure the Republican establishment for his brother. In addition to his mailing list and phone bank, Jeb had the ability to get GOP legislators on board the Bush bandwagon—by the spring of 1999, 90 of 97 Florida Republican legislators had signed pledge cards locking in support for George W.'s campaign. As Florida McCain backer Howard Opinsky explained, "There

Jeb didn't mind using his position to make his brother look good

is an inherent advantage to having your sibling as the state's chief executive." When Bush aides announced plans to have former president George Bush the Elder deliver a high-profile address to the state legislature five days before the Florida Republican primary, in which George W. was facing-off against McCain, former Florida Christian Coalition director John Dowless, said, "There's no question that the Bush family is part of the establishment and they have a lot of privileges that the rest of us don't." That was obvious on primary day. George W. beat McCain by a 74 to 20 margin statewide and, since Republicans were playing under Bush family rules, that meant George W. got all 80 Florida delegates to the Republican National Convention. By contrast, while Al Gore vanquished Bill Bradley by an 82 to 18 margin in the Florida Democratic primary, Bradley still won 31 delegates to his party's convention.

The Gore campaign looked at the Bush juggernaut and seriously considered taking a pass on the Sunshine State, but Gore's electoral mapmakers always had a hard time finding a route to the presidency that didn't lead through the big-ticket southern states of Texas or Florida. Since Texas was a definite no-go zone, that left Florida as the one Bush beachhead that might be attacked. It was with this challenge in mind that Gore selected Senator Joe Lieberman (D-Conn.), whose religious affiliation was seen as key to spiking the Jewish vote in south Florida. Gore's aides knew they would have to draw dramatic numbers of African Americans to the polls, as well.

Theoretically, Jeb Bush's years of outreach to Florida African American voters should have made the Gore strategy unworkable. But Jeb had burned that bridge just months after taking office in 1999.

Florida Democratic governors, including Lawton Chiles, had worked hard in the 1970s, 1980s, and 1990s to undo the damage done by the state's long history of slavery and segregation, developing pro-

> "There is an inherent advantage to having your sibling as the state's chief executive"
> —FLORIDA REPUBLICAN HOWARD OPINSKY

THE SHEEP IN THE HYENA'S JAW

DR. HUNTER THOMPSON

ON WHY AL GORE DIDN'T STAND A CHANCE IN JEB BUSH'S FLORIDA

This eerie presidential election has been a painful experience for Gamblers. Almost everybody Lost. Even if you were crazy or dumb enough to bet on a dead-even Tie, you Lost, because it was 537 votes short of it. The many Losers don't feel the pain yet, because they are still in Shock & Denial. There are rumors in Washington that Gore's most trusted advisors have sealed him off so completely that he still firmly believes he Won. . . . Which is True, on some scorecards, but so what? Those cards don't count. . . . George W. Bush is our President now, and you better start getting used to it. He didn't actually steal the White House from Al Gore, he just brutally wrestled it away from him in the darkness of one swampy Florida night. Gore got mugged, and the local Cops don't give a damn.

Where did Gore think he was—in some friendly Civics class? Hell no, he was in Florida, arguably the most Vicious & Corrupt state in the Union. . . . Not only that, but he was brazenly invading Florida, trying to steal it from right under the noses of the whole Bush family. It was a bold move & brilliantly done, in some ways—but then so was Lee's decision to invade the North & attack Gettysburg.

Gore was Doomed in Florida, and he knew it about halfway through Election night. The TV wizards had already given the state & its 25 precious

Electoral Votes to Gore, which gave him an early lead and caused wild rejoicing in Democratic headquarters all over the country.

My own immediate reaction was bafflement & surprise, and I think I almost believed it. . . . But not really. The more I brooded on it, the more I was troubled by waves of Queasiness & shudders of Gnawing Doubt. I felt nervous & vaguely confused, as if I had just heard a dog speak perfect English for 30 or 40 seconds. That will get your attention, for sure. . . . Some people get permanently de-stabilized by it: Nothing they see with their own eyes will ever look quite the same to them again. As in "I know that the object I'm looking at is an Egg—but I also know that if it talks to me like a person, it is *not* an Egg."

There was one exact moment, in fact, when I knew for sure that Al Gore would Never be President of the United States, no matter what the experts were saying —and that was when the whole Bush family suddenly appeared on TV and openly scoffed at the idea of Gore winning Florida. It was Nonsense, said the Candidate, Utter nonsense. . . . Anybody who believed Bush had lost Florida was a Fool. The Media, all of them, were Liars & Dunces or treacherous whores trying to sabotage his victory.

They were strong words and people said he was Bluffing. But I knew better. Of course Bush would win Florida. Losing was out of the question. Here was the whole bloody Family laughing & hooting & sneering at the dumbness of the whole world on National TV.

The old man was the real tip-off. The leer on his face was almost frightening. It was like looking into the eyes of a tall hyena with a living sheep in its mouth. The sheep's fate was sealed, and so was Al Gore's.

Dr. Hunter S. Thompson, author of one of the best political books of all time, Fear and Loathing on the Campaign Trail '72, *writes the "Hey Rube" column, which appears on the ESPN.com web site each Monday.*

grams to help African Americans get state jobs, contracts, and a leg up in college admissions. But, prodded by California businessman Ward Connerly to wipe out those affirmative action programs, Bush launched the bizarrely misnamed "One Florida" initiative. "One Florida" proved to be the most divisive development the state had seen since "English Only" groups sought to restrict the use of Spanish in official settings. Within weeks of its debut, "One Florida" had erased any inroads Jeb Bush had made into the African-American community. "The governor put us on a collision course," Senator Kendrick Meek (D-Miami) said of the Bush family and Florida's African-American voters. As Bush pushed the legislature to enact the "One Florida" plan, mass demonstrations rocked Tallahassee, with thousands chanting, "We'll remember in November." In a final effort to get Bush to rethink the initiative, African-American legislators staged a sit-in at the governor's office. Displaying the Bush family penchant for flavoring their anger with raw language, Jeb refused to negotiate with the legislators and told his aides to "kick their asses out."

Bush's words stung. And his attempts to rebuild relations with the African-American community afterward failed. In November 2000, according to exit polls and research by specialists in minority voting patterns, African-American turnout jumped by as much as 60 percent from the 1996 presidential election. Some estimates put the percentage of the total electorate that came from the African-American community at 16 percent, although African Americans make up just 11 percent of the state's population. And blacks cast 93 percent of their ballots for Gore.

"If you ask, did 'One Florida' energize and motivate the black electorate, that answer is emphatically yes," explained the Reverend R. B. Holmes, a Tallahassee preacher who had backed Jeb Bush for governor in 1998. Had George W. received the same level of African-American support Jeb had received two years earlier, the Texas Bush could have declared victory on the night of November 7, Holmes suggested. Instead, the pressure was suddenly on Jeb, the "smart" brother with all the Florida connections, to get the fix in. Fast.

> "Jeb Bush obviously wants very much to win [Florida for George W. Bush]. It's a personal matter for him. I don't know of anything more important to him."
>
> —Florida Republican chair Al Cardenas

> "I would never live it down if my brother didn't carry Florida. Imagine all the family gatherings for the next 20 years when he looked at me every time and said, 'What happened in Florida?'"
>
> —Jeb Bush

Jeb Bush was not in Florida on election night. Instead, he was in Austin with his family. Ever the cut-rate Kennedys, the comically dynastic Bushes always make a big show of family unity on election night. There's a whole routine: the family dinner, the opening of the hotel suite to photographers who capture intimate "glimpses" of New England patricians eating pork rinds, and then the round-midnight victory speech. In a family whose members have waged 25 nomination and general election campaigns since 1964, election night is a semiannual holiday celebrated with all the pomp and circumstance of Thanksgiving or Christmas.

But the news this November must have made Jeb wish he had stayed in Tallahassee.

George W. and the rest of the Bush family had been pressuring Jeb about Florida for months. In October, after the last of three uninspired presidential debates, George W. hugged and kissed the attending family members. Later, he told a reporter, "It looked like I was kissing [Jeb], but what I was really doing was whispering in his ear, 'We better carry Florida, buddy.'"

By election night, Jeb was feeling the heat.

Throughout the afternoon and early evening on November 7, Jeb and George W. were on the phone with the chairman of the Bush family's Conflict-of-Interest Department, John Ellis, the Fox television network's head election analyst who was discussing confidential Voter News Service exit polling data with his cousins. Ellis recalls a particularly anxious call from Jeb shortly after 7:52 P.M. eastern time, when Fox joined the other networks in calling Florida for Gore. "Are you sure?" Jeb asked, like a nervous kid confirming an especially poor grade with his teacher. "We're looking at a screen full of Gore," Ellis replied.

While Jeb would eventually make a farcical announcement that he was recusing himself from the Florida fight, on election night he displayed no such reticence.

Phone records show that he placed calls to and received calls from a cell phone belonging to Florida secretary of state Katherine Harris. While Bush and Harris aides dispute exactly how much contact they had through the course of the night, the secretary of state acknowledges that it was an early morning call from Jeb that woke her before dawn November 8 and sent her careening into the state Capitol office from which she would manage the recount process.

Harris had not always been an ally, but she was a smart, ambitious woman who knew how to manipulate the Florida electoral process and who knew that her own goal of becoming a key player in U.S. trade relations would be realized only if George W. won Florida and the presidency.

An early-
morning
call from
Jeb Bush
woke
Katherine
Harris

Long before Harris arrived in her office on the morning of the 8th, however, Jeb had arranged for Frank Jimenez, a close ally since 1994 who was serving as the governor's acting general counsel, to rig up a recount team for George W. Jimenez moved quickly and masterfully to make the secretary of state's office over as a partisan machine. At 3:30 A.M. on November 8, he was already on the phone to Clay Roberts, the Republican partisan who served as director of elections in Harris's office. At least eight more calls would be placed by Jimenez in the hours that followed. Before dawn, he and Roberts were plotting to prevent Attorney General Bob Butterworth, the state's chief legal officer, from playing any role in defining the nature or schedule of the recount required in a close election. Their goal, Jimenez said, was to make sure that Butterworth, a Democrat, did not "hijack" the recount. In fact, the cautious and courtly Butterworth was still making pronouncements about the need to do what was best for Florida long after Jimenez, a Cuban American with fierce Republican loyalties, had laid the groundwork for the Bush campaign's hijacking of the process.

WE READ JEB'S E-MAIL or "How do you spell 'recusal'?"

Florida governor Jeb Bush officially recused himself from involvement in his brother George W.'s fight to obtain the state's 25 electoral votes—and the presidency. By law, his staff was barred from engaging in political activity. But as is made clear by the following E-mails, which Jeb Bush was forced to release under Florida's Sunshine Law, Bush and his staff did not exactly keep the spirit of disengagement foremost in their minds during the bitter recount.

E-mail of Florida Republican to Jeb Bush (Nov. 13): "Is there any way this can be stopped? I keep getting phone calls saying 'Your vote along with 19,000 others was thrown out.'"

E-mails of Jeb Bush to Press Secretary Katie Baur and Chief of Staff Sally Bradshaw (Nov. 13, 11:00 P.M.—with previous E-mail attached): "This is a concerted effort to divide and destroy our state."

E-mail of Sally Bradshaw, governor's chief of staff, to Jeb Bush regarding the complaint (Nov. 14): "I'm working on this."

E-mail of Bradshaw to Baur (Nov. 14): "This is obscene. I hope we are getting this to the press. Shouldn't we give them a list of all the scare tactics the Gore campaign is using?"

E-mail of Baur to Bradshaw (Nov. 14): "That is what I am gathering."

Jimenez made O.J. Simpson's lawyers look like amateurs. Even as the last votes were being tabulated in the early hours of November 8, he established contact with the Secretary of State's office, making repeated calls to the Florida Division of Elections before the sun rose. It may have been the middle of the night, but Jimenez was on the clock. Around 4 a.m. on the morning of the 8th, according to published reports, Jimenez was watching CNN and noticed that the cable network had succeeded in making a live phone connection with Ed Kast, a Secretary of State's office employee, who was explaining to anchor Bernard Shaw how a recount would proceed. The definition of the recount process was not something Bush aides wanted to lose control of; pronouncements were to come only from Bush allies or Republican operatives within the Secretary of State's office, not elections specialists such as Kast. Moments after Jimenez noticed the CNN report, a confused Shaw asked, "Did we lose Ed Kast?" The connection with the Secretary of State's office had been severed.

Officially, Jimenez had taken a leave of absence from the governor's office. That was the official line. Unofficially, everyone knew he would eventually be return to the governor's office. That meant Jimenez's word was law. "When you take a leave [of absence] like that, everyone knows you're an emissary," explained veteran Tallahassee lobbyist Ron Book.

Before Jeb Bush's plane returned him to Tallahassee on November 8, his legal counsel and longtime political ally had sewn up the legal side of the recount fight. Beginning at 6:45 a.m. on the 8th, Jimenez and his aides contacted the most politically connected law firms in the state and secured their services for the Bush campaign. Calls were not placed merely to firms with Republican ties. Democratic-leaning firms, and those with bipartisan rosters of lawyers, were also contacted—in some cases to get them to jump ship and join George W's recount team. Other firms undoubtedly sensed that it might not be a good idea

"I couldn't bear the thought of sitting behind my desk doing nothing while this situation played itself out around me."

—*Frank Jimenez, Governor Jeb Bush's top lawyer, on why he took a leave of absence to aide the George W. Bush recount team in the early morning hours of November 8*

"The governor hired Frank Jimenez for his legal expertise; I don't think it's any secret he's a Republican. Skilled lawyers are a hot commodity, especially these days in Tallahassee. For all intents and purposes, he's functioning as a private citizen."

—*Katie Baur, press secretary to Jeb Bush*

"Mr. Bush's acting general counsel, Frank Jimenez, was the one who telephoned [Democratic lawyer Barry] Richard to request his services."

—The New York Times, *December 21, 2000*

"The key contribution of Bush's brother, Florida governor Jeb Bush, can also be seen: His legal staff, in the first hours after Election Day, moved to keep the state's biggest law firms off Gore's team."

—The Washington Post, *January 28, 2001*

"Last night's Florida Supreme Court ruling was a decision heard round the world. Now that tensions are high, security has been assigned to the Supreme Court spokesman Craig Waters, who called the security a precaution. The decision continues to reverberate in the Florida capitol. There the Republican legislative majority is actively trying to choose between naming Florida's 25 electors themselves or taking the case to the U.S. Supreme Court. Florida state senator Daniel Webster of Orlando gave his view of the most recent proceeding, 'Our right as legislators under the U.S. Constitution [that] solely gives us the authority to determine how our electors are chosen has been stomped on.' Governor Jeb Bush's top lawyer Frank Jimenez met with Webster, presumably giving him his boss's advice. Jimenez also met with House Majority Leader Mike Fasano."

—*Florida Capitol News Service, November 22, 2000*

"Central in the Democrats' charges is a report by the *Miami Herald* about a call from Jeb Bush's general counsel Frank Jimenez to Harris's attorneys last weekend to ask if she had issued a legal opinion about when a manual recount was warranted. Democrats charge that phone call was a not-so-subtle hint for Harris to quickly release an opinion that would not permit the recounts under way in south Florida to continue. Harris's opinion came in less than a day, and sought to stop the manual recounts in their tracks."

—*Salon.com, November 17, 2000*

for a legal group that dealt with the state to be on the wrong side of a matter about which the governor of the state cared so deeply. As one Gore operative told the *Washington Post*, long after the Democrats realized they had been outmaneuvered, "The Republicans didn't have to hire the big firms, or tie them up. They scared them shitless. Jeb Bush didn't need to send a note for them to know."

The Jeb-Jimenez combination packed a powerful punch in Florida's legal community. Among the prominent Democratic lawyers who not only did not work for Gore's side but who ended up aiding the Bush effort were Barry Richard, one of the most well connected attorneys in the state, and Joseph P. Klock, Jr. A former partner of Attorney General Janet Reno, Klock represented Katherine Harris before the U.S. Supreme Court. Klock put a team of 29 lawyers and 11 paralegals to work on Harris's behalf, running up a bill to Florida taxpayers of $627,280 in legal fees and $54,986 in expenses.

While Jimenez and the legal team locked up the legal community, another Jeb Bush operative was getting the political operation moving. Al Cardenas, the state Republican party chairman who had been one of Jeb Bush's first political backers in the state, talked to the governor on election night and instantly remade the state party as the Bush-recount-committee. The party's three-story headquarters in Tallahassee was turned over to former secretary of state James Baker and other national Bush operatives, and 30 party employees who were due to be laid off after the election were retained to assist. More importantly, Cardenas began calling Jeb Bush allies in all 67 Florida counties. The election campaign was not done, he told them; Jeb's reputation was on the line. When the party chair said that winning the recount county by county would be seen as a test of local loyalties to a governor with the power to make or break political careers, GOP county chairs and local officials got the message.

Jeb's reputation was on the line

Before "Recount One," the campaign plane carrying Gore's ground forces from Nashville to Tallahassee, had gotten off the ground, Jeb Bush had made sure that every Republican in Florida knew exactly what was expected of them. The fix was in.

Jeb himself was hunkered down with James Baker and other national campaign aides—dispensing the inside dope on all of the politicians, judges, and local officials who could be counted on to deliver for the Bush team or who would have to be isolated and shut down.

Jeb knew from the start, however, that he would have to appear to be a hands-off player. Jeb dutifully recused himself from the canvassing board that would ultimately certify the results. His place was taken by Florida secretary of agriculture Bob Crawford, a titular Democrat who had endorsed both Bush brothers in their election campaigns and who shortly after secured a high-paying agribusiness job.

Jeb walked through the motions of good governance as gracefully as he could—even appearing with Democratic attorney general Butterworth to promise a fair and nonpartisan recount on the same day that Jimenez and Roberts were talking about how best to isolate the state's top legal officer from the process.

During the 36-day battle for his state's electoral votes, Jeb kept such a low profile that most of the media stopped covering him altogether. Yet, savvy observers recognized his hand at every turn. As Florida Democratic House minority leader Lois Frankel put it, "Jeb Bush did recuse himself from the canvassing board, which I think was a good thing. But I don't think anybody should really think that he has stepped back. After all, George Bush is his brother, and you would expect him to be vigorously trying to get his brother elected. And I think behind the scenes he had been doing that."

How right was Frankel?

Savvy observers recognized Jeb's hand at every turn

Brother love: "It looked like I was kissing [Jeb], but what I was really doing was whispering in his ear, 'We better carry Florida, buddy.'"

☞ When reporters asked Jeb more than a week after the election whether members of his state staff were working on his brother's recount team, he replied, "My guess is that there are one or two people [doing so]." In fact, six high-ranking members of his gubernatorial staff had taken leaves from their state jobs to help guide the Republican recount effort. In addition to Jimenez, deputy general counsel Reg Brown and Jeb's official spokesperson, Katie Baur, logged campaign time in the days following the election. Three other lawyers from the governor's staff had taken political leaves, as well. Jimenez had taken a remarkable 64 hours of leave over the course of seven workdays. With so many Bush staffers—especially lawyers who could invoke attorney-client privilege protections—crossing back and forth between the governor's office and the recount team, Democratic National Committee aide Jenny Backus observed, "I think it begs the question of what, exactly, constitutes recusing yourself in Jeb Bush's eyes."

After reviewing E-mail traffic obtained under Florida's Sunshine Law, in which a supposedly recused Jeb Bush attacked Gore backers for seeking to "destroy the state," Gore spokesman Doug Hattaway recalled Jeb's public announcement that he would remain at arm's length from the recount. "If he is," Hattaway said, "it's a pretty short arm."

☞ Phone records reveal that Jeb's lawyer, Jimenez, placed a call to Clay Roberts at the state Division of Elections at a key point in the recount process to discuss certain types of manual recounts sought by the Gore campaign. The next day, Roberts issued an opinion essentially blocking the hand recounts Democrats wanted, costing the Gore team several critical days. As a result of the Jimenez-Roberts delay, Palm Beach County missed the recount deadline by two hours.

☞ Under the guise of concern that Florida's electoral votes not be disqualified, Jeb stirred up support for a rump move by the Republican-controlled state legislature to make a recount-be-damned declaration of the state for his brother. Though polls showed that voters were content to let the recount process continue until a clear winner had been discerned, the governor told reporters that legislators had a "responsibility and duty" to assign the state's 25 electoral votes to George W., fostering the fantasy of a constitutional crisis that did not exist.

In the end, Jeb did deliver the state's electoral votes—and the presidency—to his brother. Despite all his talk about recusing himself from the process, Jeb Bush's name can be found authorizing the Certificate of Ascertainment that was hastily dispatched to Washington after Katherine Harris certified the state's electors for George W. Bush. Jeb Bush was ultimately responsible for authorizing the expenditure of millions of state dollars to purge voter rolls on his brother's behalf before the vote. And Jeb Bush's hand worked the strings of the political and legal battle to prevent a full recount after the vote.

"If this were Yugoslavia, and at the end [of an election campaign] Milosevic was losing, you got to the last state, where Milosevic's brother was the governor, and in that state the machinery broke down, and

"It would not pass the smell test"

—REV. JESSE JACKSON

[Milosevic] won by the margin of machination in his brother's state, we would be slow to certify the election. It would not pass the smell test," said the Reverend Jesse Jackson.

Jeb Bush continues to lash out at Jackson for such remarks. "Is he a constitutional scholar in the state of Florida?" the governor demanded to know of the civil rights leader. Jeb has been similarly dismissive of the U.S. Civil Rights Commission's determination that he bore a measure of the blame for an electoral system tainted by "injustice, ineptitude, and inefficiency" and the disenfranchisement that resulted from it. Jeb rejects the commission's charge that he was guilty of "gross dereliction" of duty and that he "chose to ignore mounting evidence" of problems with his state's electoral process. The governor continues to claim he had no "direct responsibility" for anything that happened under his watch. It's a convenient out, which serves him well with the courts, the Republican Congress, and his brother's Justice Department. But no one who knows Florida, or Jeb Bush, believes this to be the case.

Trust a Republican on this issue. Almost a year before the 2000 presidential vote, Florida Republican National Committeeman Tom Slade surveyed the political landscape—atop which sat his friend, Jeb Bush—and said, "Anybody who has any idea about the [Florida] deck not being stacked in favor of George W. Bush is naive."

The governor continues to claim he had no "direct responsibility" for anything that happened under his watch

CHAPTER 8

Bush's Barristers

"The individual citizen has no federal constitutional right to vote."
—U.S. Supreme Court, majority ruling in *Bush* v. *Gore*

During the course of their careers, Chief Justice William Rehnquist and Justices Scalia, Thomas, O'Connor, and Kennedy of the United States Supreme Court had each registered themselves as supporters of the Republican Party. On December 12, 2000, they confirmed that affiliation by accepting without question—and without even the facade of deliberation—the argument of George W. Bush's legal team that a recount of Florida votes ordered by that state's highest court could not be completed.

In so doing, the five justices made Bush the president of the United States. And they made themselves into the most dubious majority of the court's 200-plus-year history.

The five partisans attempted to cloak their electioneering from the bench in the black robe of legal precedent and judicial balance. But the other four justices—including two Republicans who took seriously their duty to place the national interest ahead of political considera-

The five justices made Bush the president of the United States

tions—were not buying into the legal lie. The court's senior member, Justice John Paul Stevens, produced an emperor-has-no-clothes dissent that history will rank as one of the great rebukes of renegade jurists in the history of the republic. Because of the Court's illegal intervention, the winner of the election would never be known, Stevens argued. But the loser was clear: "the nation's confidence in the judge as the impartial guardian of the rule of law."

Along with the court's reputation for impartiality, the majority's decision also shattered the illusion that court rulings relied on reason to support their conclusions. So convoluted and illogical was the decision of the Court to rescue George W. Bush from his loser-in-waiting status that, on the December night when it was issued, no one could figure out what the court majority had determined. Network anchors, who had anxiously waited through the long night of December 11 and the even longer day of December 12 for the Court to resolve the deadlock its earlier intervention had created, broke into prime-time programming with all the bells and whistles due the biggest political story of the century. But neither they nor their reporters could decipher what the story was.

Several networks erroneously resuscitated Democrat Al Gore's campaign one last time: "U.S. Supreme Court sends recount back to Florida Court," declared CNN. Brit Hume was befuddled. Dan Rather was rather confused. Seasoned journalists struggled, on a windy night outside the Supreme Court building, to keep one hand on their toupees and the other on a thick packet of papers that made no easy sense. Even Gore resorted to channel surfing for a definitive verdict. The Laurel and Hardy of the night were NBC's Pete Williams and Dan Abrams, handing the decision back and forth to one another—hoping that, somehow, they could unlock its mystery before all of America switched to the next channel. Only when they finally reached

Brit Hume was befuddled. Dan Rather was rather confused

Stevens's clear, unblinking dissent were they able to discern the majority's intent.

The critics were scathing. In legal journals, in surveys conducted by newspapers such as the *Washington Post* and the *Los Angeles Times,* in cover stories for magazines such as *The Nation* and, finally, in books that damned the Court majority as judicial terrorists guilty of high crimes against the republic, the case was made that the Court had surrendered any claim to credibility.

Most constitutional scholars now agree that the Court should never have gone near the case. No matter what the eventual ruling, the simple act of intervention in what would otherwise have been a clumsy but wholly legitimate and ultimately sound recount represented judicial adventurism that, in the words of Georgetown law professor David Cole was "entirely unprecedented" in the history of the Court, as any resort to the Constitution, legal precedent, and the historical record should have made clear. As Justice Stephen Breyer, one of the dissenters, argued, "Of course, the selection of the president is of fundamental national importance. But that importance is political, not legal. And this Court should resist the temptation unnecessarily to resolve tangential legal disputes, where doing so threatens to determine the outcome of the election."

What Scalia and Rehnquist could not resist—"intervention by the judicial branch of government into a disputed presidential election"—had been considered inappropriate in the more than four dozen contested presidential elections that had taken place under the watch of the United States Supreme Court before the 2000 election. For two centuries, the Court had refrained from practicing election law—despite ample opportunities to enter the political fray.

Close and contested elections for the presidency are nothing new in the United States. Al Gore's popular-vote margin of victory in 2000

Most constitutional scholars now agree that the Court should never have gone near the case exceeded that of more than a dozen elected presidents, including John F. Kennedy and Richard Nixon, and it paralleled the winning margin of Jimmy Carter in 1976. Moreover, America has a long history of contested presidential results. The first real election for the presidency, the 1800 race between Thomas Jefferson and John Adams, was fought to such an inconclusive "finish" that Jefferson was not declared the winner until February 17, 1801. The contentious election of 1876, in which Florida-style disputes had to be settled in five different states, was not resolved by Congress until 4:10 A.M. on March 2, 1877—less than 80 hours before the inaugural ceremony was scheduled to take place. Even the 1960 battle between Kennedy and Nixon, which produced lingering disputes across the country, was the subject of such confusion that the last members of the electoral college were not named until January 4, 1961.

Never in any of these elections did the full Supreme Court intervene.

When a bitterly divided Supreme Court chose to take the case of *Bush* v. *Gore,* it crossed a constitutional barrier established by the nation's founders. It did so without the support of history or precedent, relying instead on a deliberate misreading of the Constitution's Equal Protection Clause and a catch-22 remedy that precluded a recount while clearly acknowledging that one was called for. This leap outside the law was made by justices who, in several instances, failed to acknowledge dramatic conflicts of interest that called for their immediate recusal.

The Court's ruling in the case of *Bush* v. *Gore* has its partisan defenders. But no argument on behalf of the Court's intervention or its decision withstands serious scrutiny.

*   *   *

Settling Federal Elections Is the Job of Congress, Not the Courts

Echoing the sentiments of the overwhelming majority of constitutional scholars who addressed the issue, Justice Breyer noted in his dissent that "the 12th Amendment commits to Congress the authority and responsibility to count electoral votes . . . Congress is the body primarily authorized to resolve remaining disputes." As recently as 1996, the Office of Senate Legal Counsel for the then-Republican-controlled chamber issued a memorandum that declared, "Courts have consistently recognized that congressional actions in this area [resolution of election disputes] present nonjusticiable political actions beyond judicial review."

Over two centuries, Congress has found many routes to resolution of disputed elections. From the repeated House votes and long negotiations that eventually resulted in Jefferson's presidency, to the appointment of the bipartisan Electoral Commission that wrestled with the 1876 race between Rutherford B. Hayes and Samuel Tilden,

RUN THAT LOGIC BY US ONE MORE TIME

"The feared constitutional crisis we so often heard about in that tense postelection period lay not in the political process spelled out in the Constitution for resolving conflicts and deadlocks in the presidential process, but in the judicial intervention and displacement of that process. We had a constitutional crisis, and it was *Bush* v. *Gore*. History will not be kind."
—David Kairys, professor, Beasley Law School, Temple University, and leading constitutional scholar

"For Supreme Court watchers, this case will be like B.C. and A.D. For many of my colleagues, this was like the day President Kennedy was assassinated. Many of us thought that courts do not act in an openly political fashion. So this decision comes as a startling event that has shaken constitutional faith. It is not that scholars cared so much about the outcome, but the way it was done. I have less respect for the Court than before. They had a chance to add to their luster; instead, they tarnished it."
—Akhil Reed Amar, professor, Yale University Law School

"One way to think about what happened is that the Supreme Court crashed in the same way a computer crashes."
—Richard Lazarus, professor, Georgetown University Law Center and director of the Supreme Court Institute

"Every four years, the United States has played the political equivalent of Russian Roulette when it has conducted a presidential election. This year [2000], the gun finally exploded."

> —William G. Ross, professor of
> Constitutional Law and Constitutional History,
> Cumberland School of Law

"The five justices clearly are criminals."

> —Vincent Bugliosi, one of the nation's
> most prominent prosecutors, writing in
> an influential article published in
> *The Nation* and subsequently extended
> to a full-length book

"This is the first time in the history of our nation that a coup d'etat has taken place within our borders."

> —Studs Terkel, Pulitzer Prize–winning
> author, who started watching the
> courts in the 1930s

"Were [the Supreme Court majority] prudent to take [the case]? I think not. . . Prudence would call for letting the political process run its course."

> —A. E. Dick Howard,
> Supreme Court scholar,
> University of Virginia

to the 1926 recount at the Capitol of 900,000 ballots from a disputed Iowa Senate contest, to the dispatch of investigators to interview several thousand New Mexico voters following a controversial 1952 House race, to the vacating of a New Hampshire Senate seat in 1974—forcing a new election to fill the post—Congress has regularly found a way to finish what voters and ballot tabulators have left undone.

Of course congressional oversight of elections has not always been a pretty process. The Senate review of fraud charges from a 1918 Michigan race dragged across three years. The Senate Rules Committee held 46 sessions and engaged in 698 roll-call votes before bouncing the 1974 New Hampshire Senate contest back to the voters of that state. There certainly have been times when partisanship prevailed. But, remarkably, majority caucuses more often than not in the twentieth century have shown little stomach for simply flexing partisan muscles to seat their allies.

Unlike the members of the Supreme Court, who deliberate in secret, hand down "conclusive" rulings that shut avenues for appeal, and enjoy the security of lifetime appointment, members of Congress conduct debates and vote under the glare of public scrutiny, are forced to consult with a second chamber, are policed by the courts, and must face the citizenry at the next election. That measure of accountability has tended to temper even the most partisan Congresses—as was illustrated in 1999, when a Republican-controlled Senate, led by such rabid conservatives as Trent Lott (R-Miss.) and Orrin Hatch (R-Utah), refused to endorse the articles of impeachment against the party's favorite whipping boy, William Jefferson Clinton.

So why didn't Congress assert its authority and take charge of the disputed 2000 election?

The Clinton impeachment crisis cost congressional Republicans a pair of House Speakers and was a factor in their loss of what had been a commanding Senate majority. As such, it left scars on the body politic. Thus, although Republican House whip Tom DeLay drew up scenarios for congressional intervention in the Bush-Gore recount, it was never a viable prospect. With the wounds of the Clinton impeachment fiasco only beginning to heal, congressional Republican leaders—and, for the most part, ranking Democrats—were in no mood to assume their responsibility to sort out a close and contentious presidential election. But had Al Gore and his strategists been wise, they would have insisted on congressional intervention. A counterintuitive move—trusting in a Republican-controlled Congress—would have given Gore the public-opinion upper hand that he and his aides might well have been able to play into a full recount in Florida.

From the start of the legal wrangling over Florida, Bush's lawyers worked to pull cases out of local and state courts and into the Supreme Court, where the majority of members had been appointed to their current positions by administrations in which the Republican nominee's father, George Herbert Walker Bush, had served either as vice president or president.

Despite frequent Republican Party tirades against "judicial activism" and Bush's campaign rhetoric about "states' rights" and "trusting the people," Bush strategists knew their man's best shot at the White House was to get the decision-making out of Florida and away from the people. They also wanted the dispute out of the hands of an elected Congress, whose members were accountable to voters. They were determined to land the case in the lap of a Supreme Court that could be trusted to deliver for the family that had shaped its majority.

> "It looks to me as though, at this stage of the game, the statute has committed the determination of the issues that you raise and the consequences that follow from them to the Congress."
>
> —Justice David Souter in response to a Bush lawyer in early December

Irrational Rationale: The Equal Protection Lie

The question that vexed the Court's conservative majority was never whether or not to construct a judicial lie in order to deliver the presidency to George W. Bush. The question was, "Which lie?"

It wouldn't do to suggest that George W. Bush had actually won. His own lawyers were effectively destroying the case for that conclusion, as they came before the Court to say they did not want any more steps taken to ascertain the will of the people of Florida.

It wouldn't do to suggest that Florida secretary of state Katherine Harris and her minions had conducted a legitimate recount of the votes cast on November 7. Clearly they had not. In fact, almost 120,000 so-called overvotes—thousands of which could be easily discerned as having been cast for Gore or Bush—had never been counted. Despite a steady spin from Bush operatives charging that Gore wanted to "keep counting the ballots until he gets the result he wants," the reality is that more than 1.5 million Florida ballots were never recounted.

Nor could the Court fully embrace the Bush line that manual recounts in close elections were unreliable. So-called hand recounts have been the accepted means of resolving election disputes since the days when Jefferson stood for the Virginia House of Burgesses. Contrary to the misguided media's impression, the Bush campaign's claim that hand recounts were prone to inaccuracy was never a serious legal strategy. It was a public relations gambit aimed at undermining faith in recounts, with the hope that there would then be less public outcry when the Court stopped the process.

No judge with any background in election law would ever have accepted James Baker's argument that "the more often ballots are recounted, especially by hand, the more likely it is that human errors, like lost ballots and other risks, will be introduced." Furthermore, the anti-manual-recount argument was rendered comic by the revelation that, in 1997, Texas governor George W. Bush had signed into law House Bill 331, which specified that manual recounts "shall be conducted" to resolve close elections. And, at the same time Republican lawyers were moving to stop the recount in Florida, they were promoting and in some cases actually demanding hand recounts of Bush and Gore votes in other closely contested states, particularly New Mexico.

> "[A thorough review of ballots would] in my view threaten irreparable harm to petitioner [George W. Bush], and to the country, by casting a cloud upon what he claims to be the legitimacy of his election."
>
> —Justice Antonin Scalia

The United States conducts more than 100,000 local, county, state, and national elections in even-numbered election years, and recounts are

BUSH CHENEY 2000 · BUSH 2000 · VOTE BUSH CHENEY · BUSH · BUSH CHENEY 2000

AUTH

WHY THEY DON'T WANT CAMERAS IN THE SUPREME COURT

common—especially at the local level where, according to a study conducted by researchers at the University of Chicago, hundreds of contests each year result in a tie or a "winning" margin of just one vote. Rare is the congressional election season in which several key races are not decided by recounts—in fact, in the same 2000 election where the Supreme Court blocked the Florida recount, control of the U.S. Senate changed as a result of a hand recount in Washington State. No serious political scientist, local election official, or secretary of state—not even Katherine Harris—has advocated for the elimination of manual recounts for the simple reason that they are a necessary, commonplace, and reliable method for resolving close elections.

Stuck for a rationale for stopping a perfectly orderly review of ballots in Florida, Scalia opted for strict application of the Constitution's 14th Amendment guarantee of "equal protection of the laws," reaching a decision that was bizarre on at least five counts:

☞ The justices who a week before had told the Florida Supreme Court not to consider equal protection concerns in developing rules for a recount were now shutting down the recount because the Florida court had not adequately considered equal protection concerns. "What the [U.S. Supreme Court] did here was like a classic pincer formation," explained Emma Coleman Jordan, a professor of law at Georgetown University Law Center. "At the first hearing, the Supreme Court declined to take up the equal protection issue. The court sent the case back to the Florida Supreme Court for clarification [on whether a previous Florida ruling had made new law]. . . . The concern raised on that issue caused the Florida Supreme Court to tiptoe around the remedy and kept it from filling in details about standards for conducting the recount. The lack of details created the equal protection issue which the [U.S. Supreme] Court ultimately ruled on. The Florida Supreme Court was damned if they provided standards and damned if they didn't."

☞ The Court majority applied the equal protection clause in the narrow context of the recount, but refused to apply it to the much broader question of whether voters in different counties were on Election Day confronted with different rules and voting systems—disparities that had a dramatic impact on whose votes counted and whose did not. "The ballots of voters in counties that use punch-card systems are more likely to be disqualified than those in counties using optical-scanning systems," argued Justice Stephen Breyer, in a stinging dissent. "Thus, in a system that allows counties to use different types of voting systems, voters already arrive at the polls with an unequal chance that their votes will be counted. I do not see how the fact that this results from counties' selection of different voting machines rather than a court order makes the outcome any more fair."

☞ Under the rationale of the Court majority, most major elections—and certainly most recounts—would be rejected as being in violation of the equal protection clause. While it can be argued that this is indeed the case, this interpretation of the clause would radically redefine the electoral landscape in a way that can hardly be described as conservative. The clear preference from the founding of the republic was that states manage their own electoral affairs. As such, even states so continually chaotic as Florida have traditionally been granted broad latitude when it comes to organizing elections and counting votes. "Every state in the union uses different procedures in elections and counts votes with different machines," explains David Cole of the Georgetown University School of Law. "Sometimes it differs by county and by precinct. In the end, this means ballots are treated differently, and they always have been. Of course, there is no intent to treat people differently, but it is the necessary result of a messy voting process. Until [the Florida intervention], no court, let alone the Supreme Court, had held these differences raised any constitutional concern, much less violated the equal protection clause. This was entirely unprecedented."

☞ Even for a Court not often accused of racial sensitivity, there was something deeply troubling about the majority's decision to use a constitutional protection designed to guarantee equal protection of the laws to freed slaves as the justification for shutting down the review of an election in which people of color suffered the most serious disenfranchisement. While African Americans make up just 11 percent of the population of Florida, the U.S. Civil Rights Commission estimates that 54 percent of discarded ballots in the November 7, 2000, election were cast by blacks. Moreover, an equal protection clause that historically has been applied to assure that citizens with limited means are accorded their full rights was used to prevent a review of ballots that were discarded two times more frequently in poor counties than in well-to-do enclaves. Of course, disenfranchisement was not a big con-

"It seems to me. . . this was a legal standard that was made up to decide this case, and this case only"
—DAVID COLE, GEORGETOWN UNIVERSITY SCHOOL OF LAW

cern for justices who had not objected on December 1 when Scalia claimed "there is no right of suffrage" in a presidential election.

☞ Finally, as its "remedy" for the possible denial of equal protection to a handful of voters, the Court offered the certainty of a denial of the franchise to tens of thousands of voters. As Jamin B. Raskin, a professor of constitutional law at American University's Washington College of Law concludes, "If voters are threatened with constitutional injury by potentially not having their votes count when similarly situated votes in other counties are being counted, that injury becomes certain and undeniable if the court orders that they not be counted."

Summing up the laundry list of legal lunkheadedness that the majority's application of the equal protection clause to the Florida fight involved, Georgetown's Cole said, "It seems to me . . . this was a legal standard that was made up to decide this case, and this case only."

Running Out the Clock:
The "No-Time-to-Count" Contradition

Scalia and his colleagues compounded the improbability of their decision with an impossible remedy. Relying on the obscure Electoral Count Act of 1887, another segregation-era relic, the Court majority suggested that December 12 was a serious deadline for selection of electoral college representatives by the states. The electoral college was not set to vote until December 18, but the 1887 law said that states should certify electors six days prior to the Electoral College vote in order to avoid disputes. Thus, the December 12 "deadline." What was not mentioned by proponents of the December 12 deadline is that electors chosen after that date would not be disqualified; they would simply be subject to congressional review—a routine measure that posed no serious threat to the recording of Florida's electoral votes.

The Supreme Court majority chose to disregard that reality, however. Ruling on December 12, the majority declared a hard-and-fast deadline had arrived: "That date is upon us, and there is no recount procedure in place under the State Supreme Court order that comports with minimal constitutional standards," the majority announced.

But this was never the case.

As Justice Ruth Bader Ginsberg argued in her dissent, "The Court's concern about 'the December 12 deadline' is misplaced . . . Were that date to pass, Florida would still be entitled to deliver electoral votes [that] Congress must count unless both Houses find that the votes 'have not been . . . regularly given.'" Ultimately, Ginsberg argued, the date debate was a joke. "None of these dates has ultimate significance in light of Congress's detailed provisions for determining, on the sixth day of January, the validity of electoral votes," she explained. Indeed, after the 1960 election, Hawaii submitted the names of its electors at the late date of January 4, 1961, and they were duly recorded.

Even assuming that December 18—the day on which the electoral college was to meet—was a hard deadline, was it still reasonable for the U.S. Supreme Court to say that the clock had run out on December 12? Most pundits and the campaign of Al Gore accepted the Court's reasoning that this was the case. A recount, it was argued, was simply too complex a procedure to undertake and complete in six days—especially if, in order to meet the equal protection standard, Florida embarked upon a complete statewide recount of all ballots cast in the November 7 election.

Even Justice Stephen Breyer, the justice with the best understanding of election laws and procedures, only hinted at the absurdity of this calculation. "Whether there is time to conduct a recount prior to December 18, when the electors are scheduled to meet, is a matter for the state courts to determine," Breyer argued.

The state courts were never pressed to make such a determination. The Gore campaign—in shock at the halt of the recount and the U.S. Supreme Court majority's clear willingness to act decisively upon its Republican bias—folded on December 13, with Gore accepting in a short speech to the nation that his options had been foreclosed.

What few cared to mention was that, by most reasonable measures, there was enough time left to set an unambiguous, constitutionally sound standard and conduct a full recount of Florida's votes.

How can we know this to be the case?

During the course of the postelection fight over Florida's electoral votes, Canada quietly conducted a national election in which voters in 301 different parliamentary constituencies across that vast country were asked to choose among candidates from a half dozen major parties and dozens of smaller political groups. On November 27, 13 million Canadian voters went to the polls—twice as many voters as in the entire state of Florida. They cast their paper ballots and by the follow-

There was enough time to conduct a full recount of Florida's votes

ing morning their votes had been counted, dozens of disputes—some of them involving extremely close results—had been resolved through instantaneous recounts, and Prime Minister Jean Chretien had already announced plans for his next administration.

Canada is not the only country with a tradition of voting, counting, recounting, and putting the election behind it in a single 24-hour period. In the United Kingdom, in June 2001, more than 25 million voters—six times the number in Florida—cast their ballots in 659 separate parliamentary constituencies for more than 2,500 candidates. Those votes were counted under the watchful eyes of observers from all the parties. Recounts, when required, were conducted on the spot. Victory speeches and concessions were delivered. And the whole process was done in time for the morning news shows to conclusively review the results.

Why couldn't Florida have done the same? Why couldn't a full recount have been conducted between December 12 and December 18? In fact, argues Pamela Karlan, a law professor at Stanford University, "If the Supreme Court was concerned about good, objective counters, they could have told the Florida Supreme Court to hire Ernst and Young or Price Waterhouse—they know how to do these things. They could have set a single standard of two chads hanging out or actual perforation and avoided the equal protection issue. But the U.S. Supreme Court did not want the Florida Supreme Court to do that. They didn't want the ballots recounted." Thus, argued Karlan, "The Supreme Court majority killed the Florida process, protecting nothing other than an outcome—Bush's victory—while disingenuously issuing a lament about its 'unsought responsibility.'"

★　　★　　★

The Court Was, to Say the Least, Extremely Conflicted

Conflicts of interest and the courts may go together like fraud and a Florida election, but the ethical entanglements of the five justices of the U.S. Supreme Court who secured the presidency for George W. Bush were epic in scope. Justices Antonin Scalia, Clarence Thomas, Anthony Kennedy, and Sandra Day O'Connor all owed their places on the Court to presidential administrations in which George W. Bush's father served as president or vice president. Chief Justice William Rehnquist began his high court career as an appointee of Richard Nixon, but was elevated to chief justice by the Reagan-Bush administration. Thomas, the only one of the current justices to have faced a significant confirmation battle, was appointed by Bush the Elder in 1991—following a series of appointments to lesser positions by the Republican administrations of the Reagan-Bush years.

None of the five justices removed themselves from the case of *Bush* v. *Gore* or attempted to provide a defense against conflict-of-interest charges, despite the fact that the federal law on recusal of jurists (28 USC 455) requires that "any justice, judge, or magistrate of the United States shall disqualify himself in any proceeding in which his impartiality might reasonably be questioned."

Other, more specific conflicts of interest that should clearly have dictated recusal were even more dramatic:

☞ Scalia, the prime mover behind the high court's decision to stop the statewide recount ordered by the Florida Supreme Court, had two sons working for law firms that represented the Bush campaign in the Florida fight. One son was a partner with Gibson, Dunn and Crutcher, the Washington firm where Ted Olson, the right-wing legal activist

Scalia had two sons working for law firms that represented the Bush campaign in the Florida fight

who twice presented the oral arguments on Bush's behalf to the U.S. Supreme Court, is a partner. Another son was working during the Florida fight with Greenberg, Traurig, PA, the Tallahassee law firm where Barry Richard, who represented the Bush campaign in the Florida courts, is a partner. The conflict was so obvious that, on the eve of the second round of oral arguments before the Supreme Court, former White House special counsel Lanny Davis suggested that Scalia should consider removing himself from the proceedings. "Under the circumstances, Justice Scalia at the very least should disclose the relationship, the presence of his son in Ted Olson's law firm, and explain why recusal, at least for appearances' sake, isn't desirable."

Davis was being generous. Under federal law (28 USC 455), a judge is required to recuse himself if he has a child who is "known by the judge to have an interest that could be substantially affected by the outcome of the proceeding." Scalia surely knew enough about the legal business to recognize that the careers of both his sons would be measurably advanced by their association with firms directly responsible for advancing the legal arguments that made Bush president—especially son Eugene, whose former partner, Olson, was rewarded with an appointment to the powerful federal legal position of solicitor general.

Yet, Scalia failed to recuse himself. (The justice failed even to offer an explanation of the conflict, as Rehnquist had when the Court ruled on an antitrust case involving Microsoft, a corporation the chief justice's attorney son had defended.) His father's refusal of recusal turned out be an even bigger bonus for Eugene Scalia than anyone expected. Several months after his father had cast the deciding vote for a Bush presidency, Scalia the younger was nominated by the new chief executive to serve as the top lawyer for the U.S. Department of Labor—a position widely seen as a stepping stone to a career in the federal judiciary or, perhaps, the post of attorney general.

Scalia failed to recuse himself

On the more political front, no member of the federal judiciary had a deeper personal interest in the ideological sea-change that occurred with the election of George W. Bush than Scalia. As a law professor and a jurist, Scalia has devoted immense amounts of time and energy to the development of the Federalist Society, a shadowy legal fraternity that identifies and nurtures conservative lawyers for appointment to federal judicial openings.

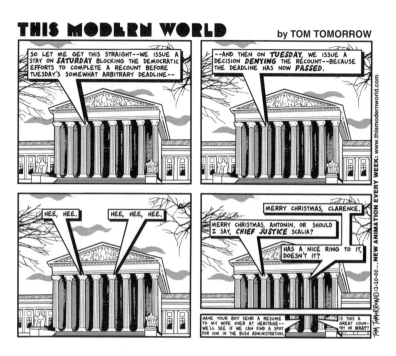

Though little publicized, Scalia's role in the Federalist Society is no secret. When the group was founded in 1982 with the express goal of forcing the federal judiciary to the right, Scalia served as one of the first faculty advisers for a Federalist Society chapter. Over the years, he has helped the group to attract millions of dollars in funding from right-wing foundations, working closely with fellow Federalist Society stalwarts Ted Olson and C. Boyden Gray to assure the success of the enterprise. Even as a Supreme Court justice, Scalia continues to lend his name to the group, appearing often at law schools across the country to personally recruit students.

The Federalist Society grew during the Reagan-Bush years and flourished during the presidency of Bush the Elder, when Gray served as White House counsel. But it hit hard times in the Clinton years, when its candidates for judicial appointments had little chance of selection. The future of almost two decades of determined work by Scalia on behalf of the group rested on the 2000 election—a Gore win would cause the group's influence to wither even further; a Bush win would rejuvenate it. (Indeed, even before the Supreme Court elected Bush, Gray was promoting a Federalist Society cofounder and Scalia protégé, Lee Liberman, as the person who should be in charge of vetting the "ideological purity" of judicial appointees by a new conservative administration.) Did Scalia "have an interest that could be substantially affected by the outcome of the proceeding"? If so, according to 28 USC 455, the federal law on recusal, he should have disqualified himself from judging the case of *Bush* v. *Gore*. Again, Scalia made no move to disqualify himself, nor did he attempt to explain why he should have been viewed as having been without conflict.

Ironically, it was Scalia who, in a majority opinion in the case of *Liteky* v. *United States,* 510 U.S. 540, 548 (1994), penned one of the Court's most pointed statements on the precise questions that arose in the case of *Bush* v. *Gore*. O'Connor and Thomas joined Scalia in endorsing the highest ethical standards. Recusal was required where "impartiality might reasonably be questioned," Scalia explained. After all, he added, what matters "is not the reality of bias or prejudice, but its appearance."

☞ Thomas's wife was employed by the Heritage Foundation, where one of her duties involved reviewing Republican résumés for the Bush administration. The federal law on recusal plainly states that a justice must disqualify himself from any case in which "his spouse . . . has a financial interest in the subject matter in controversy or in a party to

O'Connor and Thomas joined Scalia in endorsing high ethical standards, which they later failed to obey

the proceeding, or any other interest that could be substantially affected by the outcome of the proceeding."

It is difficult to imagine how Thomas's spouse would not have been substantially affected by the defeat of the man for whose administration she was reviewing résumés. Additionally, Mrs. Thomas's employer, the Heritage Foundation, is the most active right-wing think tank in Washington; no reasonable observer—and certainly no one on the public relations staff of the Heritage Foundation—would argue that it failed to benefit from a Court decision that put the White House and the extensive federal bureaucracy it controls in the hands of ideological allies.

☞ O'Connor, who has suffered from a number of physical ailments, was known in the latter years of the Clinton-Gore administration to be interested in retiring to her ranch in Arizona. But, as a longtime Republican partisan who once served as one of the party's legislative leaders in her native state, O'Connor was also known to be determined to hang on to her lifetime appointment until such time as a Republican president was in position to appoint her successor.

The prospect of eight more years of Democratic control over the White House horrified her, as it meant she would be forced to forestall her retirement. On Election Night 2000, she revealed her sentiments publicly at a party in Washington. After CBS news declared Gore the winner in Florida—and indicated that he was likely to win the presidency—O'Connor exclaimed, "This is terrible," and griped about the impact such a result would have on her personal plans. (Though Rehnquist made no such pronouncement, veteran Court watchers say that Rehnquist, long plagued by back ailments, was similarly displeased.) O'Connor's statement removed any doubt about her bias on

When she thought Gore had won, O'Connor exclaimed, "This is terrible"

behalf of Bush. As such, she should have disqualified herself under the federal law on recusal, which states that "where [a justice] has a personal bias or prejudice concerning a party," he or she must step aside.

Justice is never blind, and even the most responsible jurist may find his or her credibility questioned. Yet, in the cases of Scalia, Thomas, O'Connor, Kennedy, and Rehnquist, it is no longer a matter of questioning. There is a certainty that their conflicts—both personal and ideological—broke the bond of trust between the American people and their highest court.

Ultimately, the Bush majority has brought the Court into the broad disrepute that Justice John Paul Stevens feared. Months after the Court's ruling, at a point when aides to the new president were suggesting that the case of *Bush* v. *Gore* was "ancient history," more than 500 law professors from across the country signed a statement that began 'We are professors of law at 137 American law schools, from every part of our country, of different political beliefs. But we all agree that when a bare majority of the U.S. Supreme Court halted the recount of ballots under Florida law, the five justices were acting as political proponents of candidate Bush, not as judges."

Case closed.

"No More Floridas!"

In the 1948 film Key Largo, a gangster played by Edward G. Robinson explains the folly of attempting to clean up corrupt politics:

"You hick! I'll be back pulling strings to get guys elected mayor and governor before you ever get a 10-buck raise," Robinson rants at a Florida deputy sheriff. "Yeah, how many of those guys in office owe everything to me. I made them. Yeah, I made 'em, just like a—like a tailor makes a suit of clothes. I take a nobody, see? Teach him what to say. Get his name in the papers and pay for his campaign expenses.... Get my boys to bring the voters out. And then count the votes over and over again till they added up right and he was elected."

It is tempting to argue that nothing has changed over the past half century, especially when one imagines Jeb Bush, Tom DeLay, Karl Rove, Katherine Harris, and Antonin Scalia gathering with their minions for a good brag about how they twisted and turned the count of

"We should be able to count 100 million votes"

Florida ballots to the advantage of the failed oil man they had made over as the Republican nominee for president.

Surely, the evidence of democracy's denial in states far less swampy than Florida makes the prospect of fixing a broken system seem all the more daunting. In July 2001, researchers at the Massachusetts and California Institutes of Technology released a report detailing how as many as 6 million votes in the 2000 presidential election went uncounted because of flawed electoral machinery, human error, and intentional misdeeds not just in Florida but across the United States. It will take some industrial-strength reforms to fix a system every bit as collapsed and corrupted as the one Edward G. Robinson described in *Key Largo*.

In fact, reform is possible. Workable proposals for updating voting machinery, creating fail-safe structures to assure that no qualified voter is turned away from the polls and assuring fair and accurate counts of all ballots have been presented in Congress and state legislatures across the land. It really is only a matter of will at this point. The editorial writers at the *St. Louis Post Dispatch* put it best when they argued, "If we can count 3 billion units of the human genome, we should be able to count 100 million votes."

But will it happen? Will we give meaning to the "No more Floridas!" battlecry of election reformers? Not if we count on politicians to fix the system from the inside. Al Gore proved in Florida that, even when it is in a politician's self-interest to battle corruption, there are no guarantees that the politician will do so. Gore and his aides failed to consistently call for a full recount of all ballots, they failed to support a revote in Palm Beach County, they failed to embrace and encourage the efforts of the NAACP to expose disenfranchisement of minority voters, and, finally, they folded in the face of the Supreme Court's malfeasance that demanded not surrender but the creative counterstrategy of identifying how a recount could still be achieved.

Gore's missteps, frustrating as they may have been at the time and frustrating as they are to recall today, did not cost him Florida. The state's electoral votes were stolen by the Bush campaign and its apparatchiks in state government and the federal judiciary. That theft was made possible by a media that twisted itself to accommodate every piece of spin tossed its way by the Bush team.

These are the realities that will eventually be accepted by history as, slowly, the wall of lies crumbles. Like the journalist David Brooks, who in the summer of 2001 acknowledged that he and other conservatives conspired to discredit Anita Hill and get Clarence Thomas onto the Supreme Court, the unindicted co-conspirators of the Bush campaign and its web of official intriguers will eventually acknowledge the truth. Where will the first crack come? Already, investigators in Florida are uncovering new evidence of Katherine Harris's partisan machinations. A federal judge has given the go-ahead to a groundbreaking lawsuit by civil rights groups. Members of Congress are pressing for an investigation. Somehow, some way, someone is going to start talking. When they do, the fabric of lies will begin to unravel.

We can wait until that happens, and we can then feel good about having been right all along. Or we can act on the evidence that is already available to us. We can point to the evidence of racial disparity, systemic failure, official wrongdoing, and judicial conflicts of interest and say, "Fix this broken system!" We can point to George W. Bush and say, "You were not elected." We can point to the "Jews for Buchanan" votes and tell the defenders of the 2000 result, "Your claims of legitimacy are a joke."

We can do all this now. And we must.

Because if we do not act on what we know about the corruptions and the compromises of the 2000 election, then the joke is on us.

Resources:

Notes from a First Draft of History

The campaign for president that was supposed to end November 7, 2000, remains an unsettled affair. Rare is the day that does not produce some new twist in the storyline, some new turn of the accepted wisdom. I marvel at the impressive work of web sites such as www.democrats.com and www.truthout.com in simply keeping up with the raw material of a continuing contest. In this definitional stage, however, there is no official canon to which scholars or citizens can turn—even though lawyers, judges and law professors are doing their best to create an analytical cottage industry out of the debate over the U.S. Supreme Court's decision to shut down the vote. The core source matter for readers who seek to delve more deeply into the issues raised by the election of 2000 necessarily remains those first-drafts-of-history produced by engaged academics and by serious print, broadcast, and online journalists. Those who dismiss the academe as too choaked with ivy to meet the challenge of the moment were proved wrong in the fall of 2000 by public intellectuals who leaped at the chance to apply their knowledge and skills to the case at hand, producing essential studies that greatly expanded my understanding of everything from ballot design to the Constitution. And, while there is no question that American democracy suffered seriously in 2000 because of the neglect of basic journalistic duties and values by an increasingly corporatized and indifferent "entertainment-state" media, there is also no question that many journalists affirmed the best traditions of their craft and produced necessary investigation and analysis. The chapter notes that follow are by no means a complete review of all the necessary documentation of the 2000 campaign. Rather, these are some of the materials that underpin my take on the 2000 contest. I commend them to readers as a starting point from which to begin their own explorations, and around which to form their own conclusions.

CHAPTER 1:

Media Manipulation

First Cousin John Ellis penned a frank account of his election night activities that appeared on the Inside.com Web site (12-11-00) as "A Hard Day's Night: John Ellis' Firsthand Account of Election Night." He also gave a revealing interview to Jane Mayer of the *New Yorker* (11-20-00). PBS reporter Terence Smith produced a brilliant montage of election night coverage, "A Night to Remember" (11-08-00) for "The NewsHour with Jim Lehrer"; it can be viewed at the NewsHour's web site (www.pbs.org/newshour). A useful review of the Bush campaign's election night frenzy, "It Was a Roller-Coaster Night for Bush," by Ken Herman, appeared in the *Austin American-Statesman* (11-09-00). "Messier By the Minute," an article by Angie Cannon and Kenneth T. Walsh for

U.S. News and World Report (11-20-2000), and Jamie Dettmer's "A Wild and Crazy Election Night" for *Insight* magazine (12-04-2000) round out the picture of the Bush camp's election night. The best account of Gore's evening of uncertainty appears in Roger Simon's essential book, *Divided We Stand: How Al Gore Beat George Bush and Lost the Presidency* (Crown, New York). Some of the most revealing information about media coverage of election night came in the testimony of media executives at the 2-14-2000 hearing of the U.S. House Committee on Energy and Commerce on "Election Night 2000 Coverage by the Networks." Transcripts are in the Congressional Record or at the committee's web site (www.house.gov/commerce). A fine review of media missteps, "It Happened One Night," appeared in *Brill's Content* (2-01). Neil Hickey's "The Big

Mistake" in the January/February 2001 issue of *Columbia Journalism Review* is also useful. Finally, it is impossible to fully understand the damage done to contemporary journalism by media monopoly and bottom-line corporate pressures without reading Robert W. McChesney's *Rich Media, Poor Democracy* (The New Press).

CHAPTER 2:

Deliberate Disenfranchisement

C. Vann Woodward's history of the 1876 election and its aftermath, *Reunion & Reaction: The Compromise of 1877 & the End of Reconstruction* (Oxford University Press), and Eric Foner's exceptional book, *Reconstruction* (HarperTrade), are necessary reading for all Americans, as is Howard Zinn's reflection on the 1876 and 2000 elections in the February, 2001, edition of *The Progressive*. *Harper's* magazine offers a great review of original materials from 1876 on its web site (http://elections.harpweek.com/controversy.htm). *Mary McLeod Bethune: Building a Better World*, edited by Audrey Thomas McCluskey (University of Indiana Press) provides insight regarding Florida in the segregation era, as does *Before His Time: The Untold Story of Harry T. Moore* by Ben Green (Simon & Schuster). Jim DeFede, able political columnist for Miami's *New Times* newspaper, penned an

excellent piece on African-American participation in recent Florida elections, "Guess who's coming to vote? Guess again" (11-30-2000). The work of sociologists Jeff Manza and Christopher Uggen is essential to understanding Florida's ex-felon purge and minority-voter disenfranchisement. Their research will be featured in an upcoming book, *Locking Up the Vote: Felon Disfranchisement and American Politics* (Oxford University Press). Journalist Gregory Palast framed the story of Florida's voter purges with the article "A Blacklist Burning for Bush," which appeared in Britain's *Observer* newspaper (12-12-00) and in a BBC Television "Newsnight" report, "Theft of the Presidency" (2-16-01). Scott Hiaasen, Gary Kane, and Elliot Jaspin, of the *Palm Beach Post* advanced the story with their article "Felon Purge Sacrificed Innocent Voters" (5-27-2001), as did *Washington Post* reporter Robert Pierre's "Botched Name Purge Denied Some the Right to Vote" (5-31-01). Details about pressure from the Florida Secretary of State's office to widen the purge came out at an March 31, 2001, hearing on election reform organized in Decatur, Ga., by U.S. Reps. Cynthia McKinney and John Lewis. The most dramatic details regarding the purge and disenfranchisement of minority voters can be found in transcripts of the hearing organized by the National Association for the Advancement of Colored People in Miami on November 11, 2000. You'll find an excellent summary of the proceedings on the NAACP web site (www.naacp.org). Transcripts of two sets of hearings conducted by the U.S. Commission on Civil Rights in Tallahassee on January 11-12, 2001, and in Miami on February 16, 2001, provide a wealth of information and poignant detail. They are well summarized in the commission's report, which can be found on its web site (www.usccr.gov). A fine report on minority-voter disenfranchisement by Laura Parker and Peter Eisler, "Ballots in Black Florida Precincts Invalidated More," appeared in USA Today (4-6-01). *Los Angeles Times* writer Bob Drogin's "2 Florida Counties Show Election Day's Inequities" (3-12-01) and Julian Borger's "How Florida Played the Race Card," which appeared in Britain's Guardian newspaper (12-4-00), brilliantly illustrate aspects of racial disparity and discrimination on Election Day. Borger's piece is an example of the aggressive investigative work by British newspapers regarding disenfranchisement, which was generally superior to the reporting that appeared in American newspapers.

CHAPTER 3:
The Count That Couldn't Count

A summary of testimony by Kimball Brace and other experts on voting systems, as well as an analysis of the role different forms of voting machinery played in Florida, can be found in the U.S. Commission on Civil Rights' report, "Voting Irregularities in Florida During the 2000 Presidential Election." A report issued in March in Florida by "The Governor's Select Task Force on Election Procedures, Standards and Technology" is also useful, as is a fine newspaper report, "Voting Systems Stuck in the Past," which appeared in *USA Today* (11-13-00). The Computer Professionals for Social Responsibility Newsletter (Winter 2001 edition) featured a thoughtful and important analysis, "Getting the Chad Out: Elections, Technology and Reform," by Erik Nilsson. Research by Dr. Henry Brady and other political scientists who analyzed the ballot design and bad machinery can be found on the web (try: http://www.ssc.wisc.edu/~bhansen/vote/links.html or http://elections.fas.harvard.edu/). Brady is quoted extensively in a number of published reports, including several exceptional articles by Joel Engelhardt and Scott McCabe for the *Palm Beach Post,* the most significant of which is

"Over-votes Cost Gore the Election in Florida" (3-11-01). Anthony Salvanto's valuable analysis and related information can be found in "Ballots Offer Clues on Intent" by Tyler Bridges (*Miami Herald*, 5-11-01), "Spoiled Ballots Favored Gore" by Geoff Dougherty (*Miami Herald*, 1-22-01); and "Florida Vote Errors Cost Gore the Election," by Dennis Canchon and Jim Drinkard (*USA Today*, 6-18-01). Several Florida newspapers, particularly the *Palm Beach Post* and the *Orlando Sentinel*, have continued to investigate systemic problems that warped the Florida result. It is impossible to understand the scope of the crisis without reading the fine reports of Jeff Kunerth and Jim Leusner on caterpillar ballots and their impact on the election (*Orlando Sentinel*, 1-28-01), as well as ongoing scrutiny of discarded ballots, such as "Lake Erred by Tossing Write-ins" by David Damron and Gwyneth K. Shaw (*Sentinel*, 1- 28, 01) and "Gore Would Have Gained Votes" by Damron, Ramsey Campbell, and Roger Roy (*Sentinel*, 12-19-00). Damron and Roy broke the story of Republican "recreation" of ballots ("Mangled Ballots Resurrected," *Orlando Sentinel*, 5-7-2001), easily as important a story as the more broadly noted exposé by *New York Times* writers David Barstow, Don Van Natta, Jr., and Michael Cooper of the Bush campaign's strategy to disqualify overseas ballots for Gore (*New York Times*, 7-15-01).

CHAPTER 4:
Jews For Buchanan

Greg D. Adams, an assistant professor of Social & Decision Sciences at Carnegie Mellon University, and Chris Fastnow, director of the Center for Women in Politics in Pennsylvania at Chatham College, have pulled together an outstanding analysis of the impact of the "butterfly ballot," "Jews for Buchanan," the McReynolds vote, and most of the other strange phenomena of Palm Beach County's balloting. Their "A Note on the Voting Irregularities in Palm Beach, FL" can be found on the web (http://madison.-hss.cmu.edu/) at a site where Adams and Fastnow have pulled together some of the best academic analysis of the mishap in Florida. Among the many fine academic analyses of how the Palm Beach County ballot impacted the overall result, I highly recommend "Did More People TRY to Vote for Gore Than for Bush in Florida?" by Christopher Carroll, an economics professor at Johns Hopkins University, and "A Preliminary Look at the Vote Count in Palm Beach, Florida" by John S. Irons, an assistant professor of economics at Amherst College. Initial print, broadcast, and online coverage of the Palm Beach County "butterfly ballot" blow-up was generally anecdotal and unfocused, but John Lantigua's Salon.com feature, "Palm Beach: Ground Zero" (11-11-00) was a notable exception, as was an ahead-of-the-curve *Los Angeles Times* piece, "Bay Buchanan Sees Something Peculiar in Palm Beach Voting" (11-10-2000). Both articles disproved the Bush campaign spin about Palm Beach County being a Buchanan stronghold. Mike Lipka's "Palm Beach County Ballots Create Firestorm" (*South Florida Sun-Sentinel*, 11-10-00) put the whole mess into perspective. Philip B. Heymann's call for a new vote, "The Case for a Do-Over," appeared in the *Washington Post* (11-10-00). To read paperwork from the various lawsuits seeking a revote in Palm Beach County, visit the excellent web site set up by Stanford University's Robert Crown Law Library (http://election2000.stanford.edu/). "Judge Weighs Arguments for a New Election," by Boston Globe writer David Abel (11-18-00) offers a good review of the arguments in the revote case. For an amusing take on Ken Starr's law review reflections on voting, turn to "Would Ken Starr Call for a Revote?" by Alexander Reid and the editors of the *New York University Law Review* (*The Washington Monthly*, 11-00). "Early and Often," a column by John Seeley for the

L.A. Weekly (12-24-00) reviewed approaches used in the past to resolve similar disputes, as does the 1996 "Contested Election Cases" memorandum written by the Office of Senate Legal Counsel.

CHAPTER 5:
Homage to Katarina

The best way to begin to understand Katherine Harris's place in Florida politics is by reading E. Garrett Youngblood's short biographical essay on her grandfather, citrus millionaire Ben Hill Griffin Jr. in the *Lakeland* (Fla.) *Ledger's* "Top 50 Most Important Floridians of the Century (1998). Overseas reporters grasped the significance of Harris's old-money connections, with Indian writer Raman Swamy putting it best ("Wicked Witch of Fairy Godmother," Tehelka.com, 11-27-00) when he wrote: "In the Florida caste system, Harris is a Brahmin of the highest order, the epitome of polished Southern aristocracy." Only a handful of U.S. journalists portrayed Harris so accurately. *Miami Herald* writer Stephen Smith's "Harris' Ambitions Were Shaped by Family" (11-22-00), *Atlanta Constitution* editorial page editor Cynthia Tucker's "Florida's Harris Has Her Sights Set on Advancement" (11-19-00) and *St. Petersburg Times* state government reporter Lucy

Morgan's "Katherine Harris: Today brings an epilogue to their election dramas" (1-20-01) cut through the spin. Dana Milbank and Jo Becker of the *Washington Post* examined Harris's sordid political history with a piece headlined "Controversy Swirls Around Harris" (11-14-00). For a flavor of Harris's trade and travel obsessions, check out "Florida Secretary of State Opens Latam/Caribbean Conference" by Eric Green for the U.S. State Department's "Washington File" (12-06-00) and "Secretary of State Candidate Harris Pushes Global Trading" by *Panama City News Herald* writer Kendall Middlemas (7-28-98). A well-done *St. Petersburg Times* article by Diane Rado, "3 Caught in Glare of Electoral Dispute" (11-14-00), and post-election pieces such as the *St. Petersburg Times* editorial "Harris' Disappearing Act" (7-21-01), a *Miami Herald* exposé, "Harris's Computer Files May Be Lost: Documents Hint at Office's GOP Partisanship," by Lesley Clark and Martin Merzer (8-8-01), and a *Pensacola News Journal* editorial (8-10-01), "Harris' 'Firewall' Is Falling Apart," provide pointed reminders of the extent to which Harris politicized the Secretary of State's office. So does "Harris Sought Political Makeover" (12-22-00), a Salon.com piece by Jake Tapper, whose book on the Florida fight, *Down and Dirty*

(Little, Brown and Company) is a great read. *Washingtonian* magazine uncovered the delicious story of the Ralph Nader/Katherine Harris debate (6-01). Finally, it is difficult to argue with the accuracy of the headline on Sue Anne Pressley's well-done summing up for the *Washington Post* (1-13-2001) of Harris's testimony before the U.S. Commission on Civil Rights; it read, "Harris's Testimony on Florida Voting Called 'Laughable.'"

CHAPTER 6:
The DeLay Delay

Though Tom DeLay remains an obscure figure to most Americans, his political network has been exposed in a number of important investigative articles, including: "House Whip Wields Fund-Raising Clout" by *Washington Post* reporter Juliet Eilperin (9-18-99), "DeLay Hit With RICO Lawsuit" by *Roll Call* reporters John Bresnahan and Ethan Wallison (5-4-00), and "DeLay, Incorporated" by investigative reporter Robert Dreyfuss for the *Texas Observer* (2-4-2000). Jeff Stein's "Tom DeLay: Defender of Sweatshops" (Salon.com, 2-4-99), "Meet W.'s Biggest Problem (Tom DeLay)" by *Fortune* magazine's Jeffrey H. Birnbaum (12-20-00) and "Tom DeLay's Delectable Self-delusion" by the *Houston Chronicle* Washington columnist Cragg Hines (12-8-00) offer a taste of DeLay's fierce extremism. "Miami's Rent-a-Riot" by Salon.com's John Lantigua is the best play-by-play account of the actions that shut down the Miami-Dade count. *Time* magazine's Tim Padgett's "Mob Scene in Miami" (12-4-00) is a useful investigation of the "spontaneous" protests. A number of articles recount the involvement of DeLay's office and his minions, including a piece by *New York Times* reporters Dana Canedy and James Dao, "The Demonstrators: How the Troops Were Mobilized for the Recount" (12-28-00) and *Wall Street Journal* reporters Nicholas Kulish and Jim Vandehei's piece, "GOP Protest in Miami-Dade Is a Well-Organized Effort: Bush Campaign Pays Tab For Aides From Capitol Hill Flown in for Rallies" (11-27-00). As was often the case, much of the best reporting on DeLay's response to the election fight, and his goals for the future, appeared in the international press; Martin Kettle's report for Britain's *Guardian* newspaper, "Republican Right Challenges Dubya's Unifying Promise" (12-8-00) is a good example of this phenomenon.

. . .

CHAPTER 7:

Bushwhacked by the Better Brother

Molly Ivins and Louis DuBose do a fine job of introducing the Bush family dynamics in *Shrub: The Short but Happy Political Life of George W. Bush* (Random House). A complement to *Shrub* is an old but still relevant article from *Mother Jones*, "Bush Family Values" by Stephen Pizzo (September/October 1992). Ken Rudin, who writes the "Political Junkie" column for the washingtonpost.com web site, featured a sound review of the Jeb-versus-George debate in a column (8-8-00) where he reflected on the common wisdom that "it was Jeb—John Ellis Bush—who was supposed to be the next leader in the Bush family dynasty." *Wall Street Journal* columnist Paul Gigot has frequently explored the "Jeb-is-smarter" conundrum (*Wall Street Journal*, 5-10-99). Alan Judd, of the Tallahassee bureau of the *Gainesville Sun* newspaper produced a hard-hitting profile—"JEB! Will his pedigree carry the day?"—prior to the 1994 Florida gubernatorial election (11-94). The *Washington Post*'s Terry M. Neil reviewed Jeb Bush's transformation from combative to compassionate conservatism in a fine article: "In Fla. Race, Jeb Bush Finds 'Kinder, Gentler' Plays Well" (5-30-98), as did George Will in a nationally syndicated column, "The Developing Conservatism of Jeb Bush" (4-14-98). During the 2000 campaign, many articles reviewed Jeb Bush's efforts to maintain a low profile, so as not to outshine his brother; in one, "Jeb Bush says low profile is intentional" (Associated Press, 7-13-00), the Floridian is quoted as saying, "I don't see how I help George by having a high profile nationally. In fact, I see the opposite." During the course of the recount, most journalists accepted Jeb Bush's claim of recusal, but there were instances of appropriate skepticism, as evidenced in *Miami Herald* writer Steve Bousquet's piece, "Whoever Wins Presidency, Jeb Bush Could Be a Loser" (11-17-00) and *Los Angeles Times* columnist Ron Brownstein's "Jeb Bush Treads Lightly Amid Political Dangers" (11-30-00). Many articles detailed the active role that Bush aides, particularly Frank Jimenez, the acting general counsel for the governor, played in the recount fight; among the best of these were "6 Bush Staffers Take Leave" by *St. Petersburg Times* reporter Julie Hauserman (11-17-00), "A Wild Ride Into Uncharted Territory" by *Washington Post* staff writers David Von Drehle, Dan Balz, Ellen Nakashima, and Jo Becker (1-28-01), and "Resisting the Recount: G.O.P.'s Depth Outdid Gore's Team in Florida" by *New York Times*

staffers Adam Nagourney and David Barstow (12-22-00). Veteran Florida political reporter Mark Silva revealed important details about the partisan nature of Jeb Bush's communications during the recount campaign in an article that appeared in the *Miami Herald*, "Jeb Bush under fire for e-mail" (11-20-00).

CHAPTER 8:

Bush's Barristers

The election-related web site of Stanford University's Robert Crown Law Library (http://election2000.stanford.edu/) is a great source for briefs, trail transcripts, and other documents relating to the U.S. Supreme Court's deliberations, as well as the full text of the court's ruling in *Bush* v. *Gore* and the dissents. Veteran prosecutor Vincent Bugliosi's article for *The Nation* magazine, "None Dare Call It Treason" (2-5-01), and the book that grew out of it, *The Betrayal of America* (Nation Books) represent essential reading, as do "Bandits in Black Robes: Why You Should Still Be Angry About *Bush* v. *Gore*," by Jamin Raskin (*The Washington Monthly*, 3-01) and "A Brand New Game: No Turning Back from the Dart the Court Has Thrown" by Scott Turow (*The Washington Post*, 12-17-00). At the Institute for Policy Studies web site (www.ips-dc.org), Steve Cobble has compiled a terrific compendium of comments on the Court's ruling. (For invaluable information on electoral reform initiatives, check out IPS's www.ips-dc.org/electoral site.) Various newspapers explored the decision with leading legal theorists; the most impressive diversity of opinions can be found in the responses to a series of questions posed by *Los Angeles Times* writers David Savage and Henry Weinstein (12-00). The 1996 "Contested Election Cases" memorandum written by the Office of Senate Legal Counsel is an essential document for anyone interested in the question of whether and how Congress could have resolved the dispute. For information on foreign elections, check out the official elections web sites of Canada (www.elections.ca) and the United Kingdom (www.electoral-commission.gov.uk) as well as the web sites of the Canadian Broadcasting Corporation (http://cbc.ca) and the British Broadcasting Corporation (www.bbc.co.uk). There has been far too little analysis and comment on conflict-of-interest issues relating to the *Bush* v. *Gore* case, but Lanny Davis's comments in "Dem. Urges Scalia to Recuse Himself" (Associated Press, 12-10-00) are worthy of note, as is Joan Walsh's thoughtful commentary, "Who Will Play Daddy? Anyone Hoping the Supreme Court Would Step in and be the 'Grown-up' Got a Rude Awakening from Justice Antonin Scalia" on Salon.com (12-11-00). Finally, the web site set up by law professors who objected to the Supreme Court's handling of the *Bush* v. *Gore* case (www.the-rule-of-law.com) provides visitors with a tremendous array of resources, not least of which are the text of the advertisement the professors placed in the *New York Times* and "A Draft Resolution of Congressional Censure Against United States Supreme Court Justices Kennedy, O'Connor, Rehnquist, Scalia, and Thomas for Their Betrayal of the American People and the United States Constitution Displayed in the Decisions of *Bush* v. *Gore*."

ACKNOWLEDGMENTS

Tony Benn, the British parliamentarian and political activist who I am honored to count as my friend, says that the most important political struggle is the fight to explain that which has just happened—since that explanation of recent history creates the critical understandings upon which society will act to forge the next chapter in its development. Rarely has the struggle to define recent history been more thrilling than in the aftermath of the bitterly disputed 2000 presidential election. I was given an opportunity to wade into the middle of the fight over the Florida fiasco by my friends and editors Andy Hsiao and Diane Wachtell at The New Press. Without their support and encouragement, along with the aid of Samita Sinha, Maury Botton, and the rest of The New Press crew, this book could not have been completed on the ridiculously tight schedule we set for its production. The project benefited, as well, from fine initial research by the very wise David Deschamps, and from a thoughtful review by copy-editor/attorney-at-law Ed Davis.

Above all, however, thanks must go to my friend, Robert McChesney, who read each chapter of this book as it was written, offered wise counsel and remained constant in his faith in the project's necessity. No writer could ask for a better comrade. Thanks also to Mark Crispin Miller, Steve Cobble, John Cavanagh, Patrick Woodall, Sherrod Brown, John Kraus, John Robinson Block, Doug LaFollette, Jesse Jackson Jr., Shaun Richman, Trudy Barash, Mark Pocan, Mary Bottari, the baristas at Ancora Coffee, and countless political pals, friends, and family members for lending their insights and enthusiasm to this project. My editors at *The Nation*, Katrina vanden Heuvel and

Karen Rothmyer, as well as my editor at the *Capital Times,* David Zweifel, were flexible, understanding and supportive, as was Linda Brazill, who put up with the piles of documents, photographs and cartoons that began to fill our shared office. Melissa Ferrick, Patti Smith, Billy Joe Shaver, Joe Strummer and The Mescaleros, and the Rev. Al Green provided the soundtrack.

This book is dedicated to two women who were among the first to share with me their dissatisfaction and disgust with the 2000 election results: Margaret Bottari, who was about as good a Roosevelt Democrat as I ever knew, and Aunt Carolyn Fry, who learned her politics from Robert M. LaFollette and the good Progressives of Blue River, Wisconsin. Whenever Aunt Carolyn mentions George W. Bush, she rolls her eyes as only an 89-year-old retired schoolteacher can.

PHOTO & CARTOON CREDITS

p. ii: Rhona Wise/AFP/Corbis; p. ix: Steve Sack, *Minneapolis Star Tribune*; p. 13: Tom Tomorrow © 11-22-00, tomorrow@well.com, www.thismodernworld.com; p. 14: *The Onion, America's Finest News Source*, copyright 2000 http://www.theonion.com; p. 18: AP/Wide World Photos; p. 37: AP/Wide World Photos; p. 43: AP/Wide World Photos; p. 50: PETT © *Lexington Herald-Leader*, distributed by UNIVERSAL PRESS SYNDICATE, reprinted with permission, all rights reserved; p. 64: *Chicago Tribune*; p. 65: Joe Burbank/*Orlando Sentinel*; p. 67: Joe Burbank/*Orlando Sentinel*; p. 70: *USA Today*; p. 83: AP/Wide World Photos; p. 102: AP/Wide World Photos; p. 110: © Tribune Media Services, Inc., all rights reserved, reprinted with permission; p. 112: AP/Wide World Photos; p. 116: © 2000 Lalo Alcaraz/www.cartoonista.com; p. 126: AP/Wide World Photos; p. 131: © 2000 Jimmy Margulies, *The Record*, NJ, reprinted by permission; p. 132: AP/Wide World Photos; p. 138: AP/Wide World Photos; p. 142: AP/Wide World Photos; p. 153: Colin Braley/Reuters/Hulton Archive by Getty Images; p. 155: John Branch/*San Antonio Express-News*; p. 160: by permission of Mike Luckovich and Creators Syndicate, Inc.; p. 168: AP/Wide World Photos; p. 173: KAL (Kevin Kallaugher), CARTOONISTS & WRITERS SYNDICATE/cartoonweb.com; p. 186: AP/Wide World Photos; p. 198: AUTH © *The Philadelphia Inquirer*, reprinted with permission of UNIVERSAL PRESS SYNDICATE, all rights reserved; p. 202: Law Professors for the Rule of Law; p. 207: Tom Tomorrow © 12-20-00, tomorrow@well.com, www.thismodernworld.com; p. 210: PETT © *Lexington Herald-Leader*, distributed by UNIVERSAL PRESS SYNDICATE, reprinted with permission, all rights reserved.